GLOBETROTTER

Travel

Rowland Mead

NEW
HOLLAND

★★★ Highly recommended
★★ Recommended
★ See if you can

Sixth edition published in 2015
by MapStudio™
10 9 8 7 6 5 4 3 2 1
www.globetrottertravelguides.com

Distributed in Africa by
MapStudio™
Unit 3, Block B, M5 Park, Eastman Road,
Maitland 7405, Cape Town, South Africa
PO Box 193, Maitland 7404

Distributed in the UK/Europe/Asia by
John Beaufoy Publishing Ltd

Distributed in the USA by
National Book Network

ISBN 978 1 77026 677 3

This guidebook has been written by independent authors and
updaters. The information therein represents their impartial
opinion, and neither they nor the publishers accept payment
in return for including in the book or writing more favourable
reviews of any of the establishments. Whilst every effort has
been made to ensure that this guidebook is as accurate and
up to date as possible, please be aware that the facts quoted
are subject to change, particularly the price of food, transport
and accommodation. The Publisher accepts no responsibility
or liability for any loss, injury or inconvenience incurred by
readers or travellers using this guide.

Commissioning Editor: Elaine Fick
DTP Cartographic Manager: Genené Hart
Editors: Elaine Fick, Thea Grobbelaar, Lorissa Bouwer, Carla
Redelinghuys, Nic Orfang
Picture Researchers: Felicia Apollis, Shavonne Govender,
Colleen Abrahams
Design and DTP: Nicole Bannister, Lellyn Creamer
Cartographers: Tracey-Lee Fredericks, Nicole Bannister,
Luyolo Ndlotyeni, Reneé Spocter, Genené Hart
Consultants: Katerina and Eric Roberts
Updated in 2015 by: Lindsay Bennett

Reproduction by Hirt & Carter (Pty) Ltd, Cape Town
Printed and bound by Craft Print International Ltd, Singapore

Photographic Credits:
Axiom Photographic Library/Alberto Arzoz: page 108;
Axiom Photographic Library/Chris Caldicott: page 111;
Cover International: pages 15, 18, 25, 29, 35, 37, 38, 39, 53,
54, 56, 57, 70, 72, 73, 82, 99;
International Photobank/Peter Baker title page, pages 7, 13,
22, 24, 60, 65, 69, 71, 86;
International Photobank/Gary Goodwin: page 114;
Life File Photographic Library/Xavier Catalan: page 46;
Rowland Mead: pages 4, 27, 36, 40, 41, 43, 92, 98, 112, 115;
Eric Roberts: pages 12, 63, 89, 100;
Jeroen Snijders: pages 8, 9, 10, 11, 14, 16, 17, 20, 21, 23, 28,
29, 42, 49, 50, 51, 55, 64, 66, 76, 79, 80, 81, 83, 90, 95, 96,
104, 107, 109, 110, 113, 116, 117, 118, 119;
Shutterstock: page 84;
Travel Pictures Ltd: cover.

Keep us current
Information in travel guides is apt to change, which is why
we regularly update our guides. We'd be grateful to receive
feedback if you've noted something we should include in
our updates. If you have new information, please share
it with us by writing to the Commissioning Editor at the
MapStudio address on this page. The most significant
contribution to each new edition will receive a free copy of
the updated guide.

Front Cover: *A view from Playa Fanabe on the Costa Adeje
in Tenerife.*
Title Page: *A traditional folk-music group.*

CONTENTS

1
Introducing Tenerife

The largest of the Canary Islands, Tenerife is also the most attractive and diverse. Dominated by the snow-capped volcano of Mount Teide, the highest mountain in Spain at a height of 3718m (12,199ft), the island also has pine forests, deep ravines or *barrancos*, banana plantations, towering cliffs and arid semi-desert areas reminiscent of North Africa. Bathed by warm Atlantic waters, freshened by the trade winds and blessed by almost perpetual sun, Tenerife has been described as the 'land of eternal spring'. Little wonder that it has become a year-round tourist destination.

Tourists flock to the drier south of the island, where purpose-built resorts such as **Playa de las Américas** and **Los Cristianos** provide entertainment, nightlife, theme parks and reliable sunshine. The steady wind and impressive waves make this an ideal area for water sports such as windsurfing and sailing. Hikers, on the other hand, prefer the centre and north of Tenerife, where there is a wide network of country paths. On the north of the island stands the more sedate resort of **Puerto de la Cruz**, surrounded by old towns and luxuriant vegetation. Many visitors spend a day in the capital city and port of **Santa Cruz**. It was here that Admiral Nelson lost his arm in a naval battle.

Tenerife also has its historical towns. Just to the west of Santa Cruz is **La Laguna**, the site of the main university of the Canary Islands. Further west is **La Orotava**, with a fine collection of historical buildings and craft centres. It is set in a broad attractive valley that was much admired by Alexander von Humboldt (*see* panel, page 67).

ATLANTIC OCEAN

Lanzarote
Arrecife

Santa Cruz de la Palma
La Palma

Santa Cruz de Tenerife
Puerto del Rosario

San Sebastián de la Gomera
Tenerife
Fuerteventura

La Gomera
Las Palmas de Gran Canaria

Valverde
Gran Canaria

El Hierro

TOP ATTRACTIONS

*** Mount Teide: take the cable car up this volcano, Spain's highest mountain.
*** Parque Nacional de las Cañadas del Teide: the park around Mount Teide, full of amazing volcanic features.
** Museo de la Naturaleza y el Hombre: Tenerife's top museum in Santa Cruz.
** Playa de las Teresitas: Tenerife's best beach, composed of sand brought from the Sahara Desert.
** La Orotava Old Town: stately streets and ancient houses with richly carved wooden balconies.

◄ *Opposite: The summit of the Pico del Teide can be reached by cable car.*

INTRODUCING TENERIFE

ORIGINS OF THE GUANCHES

One of the great anthropological mysteries concerns the origin of the Guanches, the indigenous people of Tenerife. There are two schools of thought. One suggests that they came from mainland Europe, prompted by the fact that many of the Guanches had fair hair and blue eyes. The other theory, and one which is in favour at the present time, is that they came from North Africa and were of Berber origin. Whatever their background, there is the question of how they arrived at the islands, since there is no evidence that the Guanches knew how to build boats. Anthropologist Thor Heyerdahl believes that they arrived at the Canary Islands on reed boats (there is a replica boat at Güímar's Ethnological Park), but as there are no papyrus reeds on the islands, this type of boat-building skill died out.

With so much of interest in Tenerife for the visitor it is fortunate that the island has a good infrastructure of roads, allowing easy exploration. A motorway runs two thirds of the way around Tenerife, rental cars are cheap and coach excursions easily arranged. Whatever the interests of the visitor, Tenerife has all the ingredients for a wonderful holiday.

THE LAND

Tenerife is one of the **Canary Islands**, an archipelago lying some 300km (186 miles) west of the African coast of Morocco. The islands belong to Spain, which is 1120km (696 miles) to the northeast. Tenerife lies on latitude 28°N, some 480km (298 miles) from the Tropic of Cancer. In addition to Tenerife, there are six other islands in the archipelago – Gran Canaria, Lanzarote, Fuerteventura, La Palma, La Gomera and El Hierro – plus some uninhabited islets. Together, the Canary Islands cover some 7500km² (2895 sq miles). They belong geographically to **Macronesia**, a group of islands (including Madeira and the Azores) of similar volcanic origins, topography and indigenous flora and fauna. The islands began to take form approximately 40 million years ago during the Tertiary geological era (about the same time as the Atlas Mountains in North Africa) as the African tectonic plate moved to the northeast, creating a weakness in the earth's crust, out through which poured volcanic material. The Canary Islands can be thought of as the tips

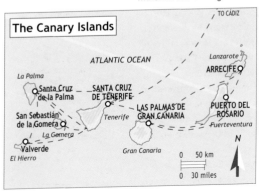

The Canary Islands

of undersea volcanoes. Looked at in this way, the peak of Mount Teide, in Tenerife, is around 7000m (23,000ft) above the sea floor. Fortunately, there is little volcanic activity in the Canary Islands today. Volcanoes are regarded as extinct in Gran Canaria and Fuerteventura. The last eruptions took place on

◄ *Left: Mount Teide is snow-capped during the winter months.*

Lanzarote in 1824 and on Tenerife in 1909. The most recent was on La Palma in 1971.

Mountains and Rivers

Tenerife is dominated by **Mount Teide**, which at 3718m (12,199ft) is the highest mountain not only in the Canary Islands, but also in the whole of Spain. It rises above the layers of clouds and seems to form the backdrop for views from all over the island. In clear conditions, Mount Teide can also often be seen from Gran Canaria and from the smaller islands to the west. In the winter months it has a capping of snow adding to its beauty, while in the summer the peak reveals layers of sulphurous ash. Around the peak is a huge depression called Las Cañadas, which is a caldera or collapsed crater. Nearby volcanic peaks include **Pico Viejo** (3135m/10,285ft) and **Montaña Blanca** (2750m/9023ft), while to the northwest is **Volcán Negro** (1626m/5335ft), the lava of which was responsible for devastating the northern port of Garachico in 1706. The most recent volcanic activity occurred in 1909, when **Mount Chinero**, to the northwest of Teide, poured out lava for 10 consecutive days. The volcanoes of the Teide complex are now dormant but geologists consider that further eruptions during the 21st century are a possibility.

A rocky volcanic ridge, known as the **Cumbre Dorsal**, leads to the northeast from Teide forming a backbone for most of

THE ORIGIN OF CANARY

Controversy has always raged about the origin of the name 'Canary'. True, there are wild canaries throughout the archipelago, but these birds probably got their name from the islands, rather than the other way around. A popular theory is that early settlers were impressed by the size of the dogs on the islands and used the Latin word for dogs (*canus*) to name the area. A further supposition is that the primitive inhabitants were Berbers from the Canarii tribe in Morocco. Take your pick!

PLATE TECTONICS

The theory of **Plate Tectonics** explains the distribution of the world's volcanoes. Derived from the **Theory of Continental Drift**, it shows that the earth's crust is divided into moveable plates. The plate boundaries are lines of weakness through which volcanic magma pours. This explains volcanoes in the mid-Atlantic where the American and European plates are moving apart. The Canary Islands are not on the mid-Atlantic ridge, but lie in an area of the crust's weakness caused by the movement that has built up the nearby Atlas Mountains in North Africa, as the African plate has drifted eastward.

INTRODUCING TENERIFE

▲ *Above: Puerto de la Cruz is a stylish resort on the cloudier north of the island.*

the island. Occupying the tip of the peninsula, north of the capital Santa Cruz, are **Las Montañas de Anaga**. These basalt mountains are the result of one of the early lava flows and are, geologically speaking, the oldest part of Tenerife.

There are no permanent river courses in Tenerife, but there is evidence everywhere of erosion by rivers. Deep valleys run in a radial pattern from the highest points on the island, but running water is only found in them after winter rains or melting snow. These dry valleys, or *barrancos*, were probably formed during wetter periods of geological time.

A different type of landscape is found on the eastern side of Tenerife, where the low rainfall and lack of trees has created an area of arid **semi-desert**, which has much in common with North Africa, located some 300km (186 miles) to the east.

Seas and Shores

Tenerife is surrounded by the deep waters of the **Atlantic Ocean**. Its erosive power shapes the coastline and over geological time the waves have worked on the volcanic rocks producing Tenerife's varied shoreline. The eastern coast is generally low-lying, but the remainder of the island has some spectacular cliffs, notably those in the west at **Los Gigantes**, which rise almost vertically to over 600m (nearly 2000ft). Tenerife's beaches are generally disappointing. Often they consist of unattractive black volcanic sand, although in places such as **Playa de las Teresitas**, near Santa Cruz, vast amounts of golden sand have been imported from the Sahara Desert. The lack of decent beaches is not, however, a handicap, as most apartments and hotels have excellent pools and in some other areas, such as **Puerto de la Cruz**, sea-water lido complexes have been built. Tenerife's Atlantic shoreline also ensures that almost every conceivable type of **water sport** can be catered for, including surfing, sail boarding, deep-sea fishing and scuba diving.

Climate

The climate of Tenerife has been described as that of 'per-petual spring', although it can be more like continual sum-mer in some of the island's more southerly resorts. There is, in fact, considerable climatic variety on the island depending on geographical position and the height of the land. The moist **trade winds** blow from a northeasterly direction, so that the windward northern coasts have more rain and cloud than the rest of the island. The leeward south and southwest of Tenerife are drier and hotter. These areas may have as much as 2500 hours of **sunshine** a year, and it is here that recent tourist development has concentrated. **Temperatures** vary from 18 to 24ºC (65 to 75ºF) in the summer and 16 to 20ºC (61 to 68ºF) in the winter, although afternoon tem-peratures during both seasons can be considerably higher. Occasionally in the summer the hot sirocco wind blows from the Sahara bringing desert dust, high temperatures and discomfort to all. **Rainfall** is generally light and varies from 750mm (29.5in) on the north coast to 250mm (9.8in) in the southwest. One interesting feature of the Tenerife climate is the layer of **cloud**, which, brought by the trade winds, lies on the windward side of the island between 500m (1650ft) and 1500m (4920ft). It may burn off during the afternoon, but can last for days, providing light rain for agriculture. The final climatic factor is the cool **Canary Current**. This flows from the north, ensuring that the sea tem-peratures around the island are lower than might be expected for this latitude: around 18ºC (64.5ºF) in the winter, and rising to 22ºC (71ºF) in the summer.

Flora and Fauna

The varied altitude levels, the rich volcanic soil and the amenable climate combine to make Tenerife a botanist's paradise. There are a huge number of plants which are

▼ *Below: The bird-of-paradise flower or strelitzia is widely found in parks and hotel gardens.*

INTRODUCING TENERIFE

indigenous to Tenerife. To this list can be added the species of Mediterranean origin, brought in by the Spaniards after the Conquest, plus exotic plants brought to Tenerife by sailors and travellers from all over the world.

In the arid semi-desert areas in the south of the island, drought resistant plants form scrubland. Especially common are the euphorbias or **spurges**. Growing widely are the candelabra spurge (which looks very much like a cactus) and the various species of Canarian spurge. The south of Tenerife also has large areas of crops cultivated under plastic, including tomatoes and bananas, grown with the aid of irrigation water. In the wetter north, the lower levels are characterized by a wide variety of tropical crops including oranges, dates and sugar cane. The towns, cities and hotel gardens are bright with introduced flowers and shrubs such as bougainvillea, hibiscus, geraniums and strelitzia (or bird-of-paradise flower), plus colourful trees such as jacaranda and mimosa.

At higher levels, where cloud is more frequent, Canarian pines, eucalyptus and cork oak are common, while Poinsettias grow like weeds along the roadsides. Under these conditions crops such as grapes, potatoes and cereals thrive. In the **Anaga Mountains** in the northeast of the island is one of the last remaining stands of Canarian laurel, with associated heather, holly and linden. The highest part of Tenerife is the area around Mount Teide, known officially as the **Las Cañadas del Teide National Park**. This is the home of the hardy Teide violet and the remarkable Teide viper's bugloss or *tajinaste*, which every two years produces a metre-long spike of dramatic red flowers. No account of Tenerife flora would be complete without a mention of the remarkable **Drago Milenario** (*Dracaena draco*). Some specimens reach an impressive 18m (59ft) in height and can live for hundreds of years.

▼ *Below: A viewpoint in the Anaga Mountains gives a fine vista along the northeastern coastline.*

In contrast to the flora, the animal life of Tenerife is disappointing. Only 56 species of **birds** have been recorded as breeding in Tenerife; some have become extinct and many are only spasmodic breeders. Bird-watchers will be keen to see three species which are endemic to the Canary Islands – the blue chaffinch, the white-tailed laurel pigeon and the Bolles laurel pigeon. The last two are extremely rare. In addition, there are three Macronesian endemisms – the plain swift, Berthalots pipit and the wild canary – all of which are reasonably common. The only frequently seen raptors are kestrels, sparrowhawks and buzzards. Other common birds are Spanish sparrows, blackcaps, chiffchaffs, hoopoes and blackbirds. The visitor may also be surprised to see small flocks of noisy parrots that have escaped from theme parks and are able to survive well in the wild. All in all, Tenerife is not a noted ornithological site.

▲ Above: The large Canarian lizard is often seen in the crevices in stone walls.

Amongst the **amphibians** and **reptiles** there are two frogs, three geckoes, a lizard and a skink. Geckoes are often found in houses, clinging to walls and ceilings where they deal effectively with insects and are regarded by the locals as signs of good luck. The large Canarian lizard, of which there are three subspecies in Tenerife, is abundant in stone walls, where it feeds on insects and plants.

With the exception of bats, all terrestial **mammals** in Tenerife were introduced by humans. There are six bats and all but one are common. Rabbits, house mice, hedgehogs and black and brown rats have been around for some time. The pygmy white-toothed shrew was first discovered in Tenerife in 1983 and has now spread over much of the island. It is the main source of food for buzzards and kestrels. Another recent introduction has been the moufflon, which was released in the Las Cañadas del Teide National Park in 1971. However, research has shown that it is a serious threat to the indigenous flora and its numbers are now being controlled. **Marine mammals** are well represented and include a number of species

THE CHRISTMAS WEED

Growing along the verges of the rural roads of Tenerife are huge stands of **Poinsettia** (*Euphorbia pulcherrima*). This is surprising to the visitors from northern Europe, who normally associate the Poinsettia with potted plants at Christmas. In Tenerife, however, it grows almost like a weed. Originally from Mexico, it can reach heights of 2m (6.5ft). On top of the woody stems are small insignificant yellow flowers, surrounded by bright red leaves (which are often mistaken for the flowers).

INTRODUCING TENERIFE

▲ *Above: Wild dolphins can be seen in the ocean around Tenerife. These captive specimens give displays at Loro Parque near Puerto de la Cruz.*

of whale, porpoise and dolphin. Over 400 species of **fish** have been noted in the waters surrounding Tenerife. They include types of shark, tuna, stingrays and many of the fish that turn up on the menus in restaurants, such as hake, sardines and swordfish. Common shellfish include lobsters, prawns and mussels.

There is a wide range of **insects**, including the unwelcome mosquito. A few dragonflies are in evidence in the wetter areas, including the common scarlet darter. Among the endemic butterflies are the Canarian versions of the red admiral, grayling, speckled wood and cleopatra. Migrating monarchs can be abundant at certain times of the year.

HISTORY IN BRIEF

The early history of the Canary Islands is shrouded in myth and mystery. The Greeks and the Romans certainly knew of their existence. Plato thought that they were the remains of the lost continent of Atlantis, while the geographer Ptolemy accurately located their position in AD150. It is highly unlikely, however, that either the Greeks or the Romans set foot on the Canary Islands. On the other hand, the Phoenicians and the Cathaginians almost certainly did.

Early Inhabitants

Remains of **Cro Magnon Man** have been found on the Canary Islands. Examination of skulls showing people with broad faces and high foreheads, have been carbondated as ca. 3000BC. When European exploration of the islands took place in the 14th century, they found primitive people living there who were tall, blond and blue-eyed. They were known on Tenerife as **Guanches**, a name that is now applied to the early inhabitants of all the Canary Islands. Nobody is really certain of their origins (although most experts believe they were Berbers from North Africa) or how they got to the islands, as they appear to have had no knowledge of boat building.

DRAGO MILENARIO

Of all the trees in Tenerife, it is the **Drago Milenarion** (Dragon tree) (*Dracæna draco*) that is the most interesting and mysterious. The tree is believed to live for several centuries, but a precise dating is impossible as it does not produce tree rings. The tree has survived the Ice Age and is a remnant of the Tertiary era flora. Traditionally, Guanche meetings took place under a Dragon tree. They also used its sap (predictably called 'dragon's blood', as it turns bright red on exposure to air) to heal wounds, ward off evil spirits and to embalm their dead. The sap is also believed to be a cure for leprosy, and for a time it was exported to Italy to stain marble and violins.

HISTORICAL CALENDAR

3000BC–AD1500
Archaeological evidence from skulls suggests the island was inhabited by Cro Magnon Man.

1100BC Phoenicians and Carthaginians are believed to have visited the Canary Islands.

1312 Genoese explorer Lanzarotto Malocello occupies and names Lanzarote after himself.

1340 Portugal and Spain send ships to investigate the islands, finding Guanches living a Stone Age existence.

1401 Spanish Conquest begins with Jean de Béthancourt taking Lanzarote, followed swiftly by La Gomera and Fuerteventura.

1478 Juan Réjon attacks Gran Canaria, but takes a further five years to subdue the Guanches.

1483 Pedro de Viera is appointed as the first Governor of the Canary Islands.

1492 Columbus makes his first visit to the Canary Islands and observes Mount Teide erupting.

1494 Tenerife is the last island to fall to the Spanish forces.

16th and 17th centuries
The Spanish colonize the islands with the settlers developing a thriving economy, aided by the slave trade.

1657 Admiral Blake destroys a Spanish treasure fleet near Santa Cruz.

1797 Admiral Nelson's attempt to take Santa Cruz is repelled.

1852 Isabella II declares the Canary Islands a free trade zone.

Late 19th century Bananas replace sugar cane as the mainstay of the Canary Islands'

economy.

1927 Canary Islands divided into two provinces, with Santa Cruz named the capital of the western province.

1936 General Franco plots a military coup in Tenerife, which leads to the onset of the Spanish Civil War.

1982 Regional constitution granted by Spain to the Canary Islands.

1986 Canary Islands gain special status within the European Union.

2002 Introduction of the euro.

2007 Tenerife tram opens with services around Santa Cruz and to La Laguna.

2013 Heavy rain in December causes flash floods that kill five people.

2014 Spanish oil company Repsol begins exploration in the waters of the Canary Islands, despite local protests.

Guanche Society

Early European settlers found a primitive Stone Age society, with no knowledge of metals, the wheel, boat building or the bow and arrow. The majority lived in caves, although a few high-status Guanches had stone houses with straw roofs. Their economy was based on cattle rearing and the growing of crops. The women made pots that were highly decorated, using the coil method rather than the wheel. Clothing was made from sheep or goatskins. These animals also provided meat, cheese and milk. The Guanches also ate fish, fruit and *gofio*, which was roasted cereal flour.

Despite their primitive way of life, the Guanches had a sophisticated social structure. Tenerife was di-

▼ *Below: A Guanche Park exhibit displaying the early inhabitants' way of life.*

INTRODUCING TENERIFE

FACTS AND FIGURES

Size: 2057km² (794 sq miles)
Population: 908,000 (2012)
Capital: Santa Cruz is the capital of both Tenerife and the western province of the Canary Islands. Population 206,000.
Position: 300km (186 miles) west of the African coast, 17°W and 27°N.
Time Zone: Follows GMT
Language: Spanish
Religion: Roman Catholic
Highest Mountain: Mount Teide at 3718m (12,199ft)
Tourism: Five million visitors per annum, providing 60 per cent of GNP.

vided into nine kingdoms, each ruled by a mencey who was advised by a council of nobles known as a *tagoror*. The council usually met under an ancient Dragon tree, from where they administered justice. The Guanches were monogamous and women played a full part in society. There was no death penalty, but murderers were severely beaten and their possessions given to the relatives of their victims as compensation. The Guanches worshipped a god known as **Achaman**, who was closely linked with the sun, while Hell was believed to be in the Teide volcano. They also mummified their dead from the highest social strata, using skins and reeds, before laying them in special burial caves.

The Spanish Conquest

The conquest of the Canary Islands by the Europeans began in 1312, when a Genoese explorer **Lanzarotto Malocello** conquered, and gave his name to, Lanzarote. Then followed years of squabbling between Spain and Portugal over the theoretical ownership of the islands, ending in 1401 with the islands being incorporated into the Spanish crown. European conquest began in earnest the following year when **Jean de Béthancourt** took Lanzarote for the King of Castile. By 1406 Béthancourt had also conquered Fuerteventura and La Gomera. Little further progress was made in the face of some determined Guanche resistence. Spain began a second phase of the Conquest in 1478, when Ferdinand and Isabella sanctioned an attack on Gran Canaria by **Juan Réjon**. He met fierce resistance and it was five years before the local Guanches were subdued. The next Spanish commander on

▼ *Below: This reconstruction of a reed boat is on display at Güímar's Ethnographical Park.*

the scene was **Alonso Fernández de Lugo**, who in 1491 received royal assent to attack La Palma and Tenerife. La Palma was quickly taken, but Tenerife was to prove the toughest island to overcome. De Lugo landed near the present day Santa Cruz in May 1493 with a force of 1000 soldiers plus 150 Guanche mercenaries from Gran Canaria. De Lugo negotiated with the nine *menceyes*, some of whom gave in peacefully. He then moved in on the remaining tribes, but his forces were ambushed in the Barranco de Acentejo, suffering heavy losses. De Lugo went to Spain, recruited more men and returned to Tenerife later in the year. He had more success in a battle at La Laguna in November 1494, but the Guanche's resistance was far from over. Fortunately for de Lugo, a plague decimated Guanche numbers. The demoralized survivors were defeated at the second battle at Acentejo and the conquest was, to all intents and purposes, over.

▲ *Above: Bronze statues of Guanche leaders line the promenade at Candelaria.*

Post-Conquest Guanches

After the Conquest, Tenerife and its colonists were administered for Spain by *capitanes-generales*. Many Guanches died from diseases introduced by the newcomers, to which they had no resistance. Large numbers of the Guanches were taken to Spain as slaves (although many were later allowed to return). Others interbred with the invaders, assumed Spanish names and were converted to Christianity. Assimilation with the colonists came swiftly and the Guanche's spoken language quickly disappeared. However, anthropological research with DNA shows that many of the Guanches characteristics are retained by modern Canarians. Certainly a great number of the inhabitants of Tenerife are proud of their Guanche ancestry, as they like to feel that this highlights the differences between themselves and the mainland Spaniards.

VERDINO DOGS

It is often claimed that the Canary Islands were named for the Latin *canus*, meaning 'dog'. Records mention large dogs found on the islands, and some researchers suggest that the inhabitants actually ate dogs. Certainly, the Conquistadors found that the Guanches kept dogs to guard their flocks. The invaders feared the dogs and passed a law allowing each shepherd only one dog. Known as *verdinos* for their greenish tinge, the dogs were smooth-haired with broad jaws. Today, as part of the revived nationalism of the *Canarios*, there is a movement to keep the Verdino strain pure and have it confirmed as a registered breed.

INTRODUCING TENERIFE

▲ *Above: Vineyards in the north of the island; the peak period of wine production was in the 18th century.*

Spanish Colonial Rule

For the next three centuries, the Canary Islands experienced mixed fortunes under Spanish colonial rule. The islands attracted large numbers of settlers, not only from Spain, but also from Portugal, France and Italy. After Columbus's discovery of the New World in 1492, the Canary Islands became an important staging post for ships travelling to and from the Americas. Any territory owned by Spain, however, was fair game for corsairs and the Barbary pirates who frequently raided the islands. The fleets of Britain, France, Holland and Portugal made numerous attempts to take the Canaries, without lasting success. There were some spectacular British naval engagements off Tenerife. In 1657, Blake totally destroyed a Spanish treasure fleet near Santa Cruz. Nelson was less fortunate in 1797 when he not only failed to subdue Santa Cruz, but lost his right arm in the battle as well.

Boom and Bust

During the years of colonial rule, the Canary Islands in general and Tenerife in particular, experienced varied economic fortunes. Reliance on various types of monoculture led to cycles of 'boom and bust', with the downturns leading to mass emigration to the New World. In the early 16th century, **sugar cane** was introduced from Asia. The industry was able to use slave labour and sugar became Tenerife's main source of income. The abolition of slavery in 1537 and the cheaper sugar produced in Brazil and Central America led to the collapse of the industry. The cultivation of sugar cane was replaced by the production of **wine**, particularly on Tenerife. The vines produced a strong sherry-like wine known as 'malmsey' or what Shakespeare referred to as Canary Sack. It was very popular in Elizabethan England and at the height of its production some 10,000 barrels were sent to London annually. Many of the fine buildings in the historic towns of Tenerife were constructed on the profits of the wine trade.

Unfortunately, the success of the wine trade was not to last. Changing tastes, disease of the vines and the success of the rival Madeira wine meant that by the start of the 19th century, the wine boom was over. This led inevitably to further emigration, mainly to Venezuela and Cuba.

In 1825, a new product came on the scene. This was **cochineal**, a red dye that was extracted from a small insect which was parasitic on cactus plants. Thousands of prickly pear cactus plants soon appeared in many parts of Tenerife as this unusual type of farming boomed. By the 1870s, however, chemical dyes began to appear on the market and the cochineal trade fell away. More emigration!

Meanwhile, there were important political developments. The Canary Islands were declared a province of Spain in 1821, with Santa Cruz de Tenerife named the capital. Inter-island rivalry was never far from the surface and in 1912 Spain introduced Island Councils or *Cabildos*. In 1927 the Spanish Government divided the Canary Islands into two provinces – an eastern province comprising Lanzarote, Fuerteventura and Gran Canaria, with its capital at Las Palmas, and a western province made up of Tenerife and the smaller islands of La Gomera, El Hierro and La Palma, with the capital at Santa Cruz de Tenerife.

The economy of the Canary Islands showed an upturn during the late 19th and early 20th centuries, helped by their designation as a free trade zone and the growth of the Atlantic steamship trade. In the 1850s, British entrepreneurs introduced banana production to the islands, and by the turn of the century there were banana plantations across many of the wetter parts of Tenerife. Although bananas are still produced in Tenerife today, the disruption caused by two world wars and the competition from Central and South America

BATTLE OF NELSON'S ARM

It is probably true to say that few of the thousands of English tourists who visit the Canary Islands annually, realize that their national hero, Admiral Horatio Nelson, lost a battle (and his arm) in a naval engagement at Tenerife. After the Spanish Conquest and the discovery of the Americas, the Canary Islands enjoyed a period of prosperity. This made ports, such as Santa Cruz de Tenerife, a popular target for both pirates and the ships of rival seafaring nations. In 1797, Nelson was instructed to seize the port. His assault, however, was a failure, due to rough seas and the staunch defence of the townspeople. During the battle, Nelson lost his right arm to cannon fire. His flotilla escaped, and this was Nelson's only defeat in an illustrious career.

▼ *Below: Lush banana plantations are found in the wetter parts of the north of the island.*

INTRODUCING TENERIFE

led to a slump in production. The result was a further wave of emigration to the Americas. The extent of this emigration is illustrated by the fact that over a quarter of a million people of Canary Island origin are estimated to live in Caracas, the capital of Venezuela.

The Rise of Franco

During the 1930s, Tenerife found itself involved in the Spanish Civil War. In March 1936, General Franco – who was suspected of planning a coup to overthrow the government – was 'exiled' to Tenerife with the post of *Commandante-General*. Franco was on Tenerife for a mere four months, but during this time he survived no fewer than three assassination attempts while he planned his next coup. The action began in Morocco, and Franco quickly flew there to lead the insurgents. Thus began the brutal Civil War that was to divide towns and families. Two days after Franco's departure, the fascists took control of Tenerife.

The Growth of Tourism

Despite Spain's historic links with Tenerife, the Canary Islands were largely neglected during Franco's years in

▼ Below: Memorial to those who fell in the Spanish Civil War. The monument is located in the Plaza de España in Santa Cruz.

power, giving rise to an active separatist movement in the archipelago. The movement was only stemmed in 1982, when the Canaries (and other parts of Spain) were given autonomous powers and a regional constitution. Another factor that quelled nationalism was the growth of **tourism**, which is now Tenerife's main source of convertible revenue.

▲ *Above: The colours of the Canary Islands' flag were taken from the naval flags of Santa Cruz de Tenerife and Las Palmas.*

GOVERNMENT AND ECONOMY
Government

The two provinces of the Canary Islands form one of the 17 autonomous regional communities in Spain. Rivalry between the islands is traditional and the regional government has offices in both Santa Cruz de Tenerife and Las Palmas on Gran Canaria. The regional government has powers covering transport, agriculture, health and policing, and can raise local taxes. Each island has a local administration (the *cabildo*), while a further level of administration known as the district or *municipio* is also in place.

The main **political parties** are the left wing Partido Socialista Obrero Español (PSOE) and the right of centre Partido Popular (PP). In the 1990s the various nationalist groups merged to form the Coalición Canaria (CC) which, rather than pressing for independence, now works for a better deal from Madrid. Recent governments have been a coalition between the Partido Socialista Obrero Español, the Coalición Canaria and Partido Popular.

The Economy

Canarian **agriculture** has learnt that monoculture does not pay in the long run, and most farms have a variety of enterprises. Crops here include bananas, tomatoes, tobacco, coffee, citrus fruit and exotic fruits and flowers. Animal husbandry is quite rare and confined to a few goats, sheep and cattle. Agricultural production is helped by the fertile volcanic soil, the equable climate and the use of plastic greenhouses

BERTHALOT'S PIPIT

This unassuming little brown bird is endemic to the Canary Islands and found in dry places from sea level to the higher parts of Mount Teide. It is often seen on the ground in small family groups seeking insects, and will allow people to approach quite closely before flying off. But how did it get its strange title? It was, in fact, named by Sabin Berthelot, the French Consul in Santa Cruz, who introduced bananas and cochineal to the island in the 19th century. He also collaborated with the British naturalist FB Webb to write the *Natural History of the Canary Islands*.

and irrigation. Water supply is a constant problem these days, as precipitation totals have dropped and the demands of tourism have increased. Much use is made of volcanic clinker to conserve soil moisture levels.

The **manufacturing industry** accounts for only 9 per cent of the island's GDP. Tax discounts are designed to attract business to the island and IVA (the Spanish equivalent of VAT) is only 7 per cent, compared with 21 per cent on the mainland. The **tertiary sector** of industry is dominated by **tourism**. The Canary Islands are an all-year-round destination attracting over 10 million visitors annually, mainly from Britain, Germany, Scandinavia, Holland and mainland Spain. This income has had the effect of improving the island's infrastructure to the benefit of *Canarios* and visitors alike. Nevertheless, unemployment figures are high at 33 per cent and average wages are among the lowest in the EU. The economy of the Canary Islands is currently boosted by several billion euros annually due to its status as one of the EU's Ultra-Peripheral Regions (UPRs).

WOODEN BALCONIES

There is a long tradition of wood carving in Tenerife that is shown to good advantage in the Plateresque style used widely in churches during the 16th and 17th centuries. With plenty of Canarian pine available, it was inevitable that the style would spread into domestic architecture. The pine is easily carved but also very durable and best seen in the intricately carved balconies of the fine mansions of the country, particularly in the older parts of La Laguna and La Orotava.

THE PEOPLE

The total **population** of the Canary Islands currently stands at 2,07 5,000 and grows at more than 1 per cent annually. At the last census in 2008, Tenerife had 899,833 inhabitants, including a good number of foreign residents, mainly from Britain and Germany. There are also small numbers from the Americas, mainly returning emigrants from countries such as Cuba and Venezuela. The people from Tenerife are known locally as *tinerfeños*. They are mainly descended from Spaniards and are generally dark haired with an olive complexion. They are fiercely patriotic, regarding themselves as *Canarios*, rather than from the *peninsular* as they call mainland Spain. They have mixed feelings towards mainland Spaniards, calling them *godos* (or Goths) and accusing them of taking local jobs. Indeed many *Canarios* like to think of themselves as African rather than Spanish.

Like the mainland Spanish, *Canarios* are family-orientated. Machismo is still a feature of male life, but women have become increasingly liberated and now take a full part in public life, with many being employed in the tourist industry.

Language

The official language on Tenerife is **Castilian Spanish**, but pronunciation is more akin to Spanish spoken in Andalucía or South America. The lisping 'th' applied to 'c' and 'z' is replaced by an 's' sound. Consonants at the ends of words are often omitted, so that *gracias* becomes *gracia*. Some words borrowed from South American Spanish are in common use, such as the Cuban *gua gua* (pronounced *wah wah*) for autobus. *Tinerfeños* always appreciate an attempt to speak their language, so bring a good phrase book and dictionary.

Some **Guanche** words have survived, mainly in place names. **English** is widely spoken in the tourist industry.

EMIGRATION

Throughout the history of the Canary Islands emigration has been a continuing theme, usually coinciding with downturns in the economy. Ships crossing the Atlantic frequently stopped to refuel in the Canary Islands and it was easy to book a passage. The usual destination was Latin America, where Spanish was universally spoken. A favourite destination in the early years was Cuba where emigrants from the Canaries played an important role in the growth of the capital, Havana, and in the development of the cigar-making industry. During the difficult days of the Spanish Civil War, and later World War II, there was renewed emigration, this time to Venezuela. However, with the growth of tourism there has been plenty of work and little need to emigrate. In fact, many northern Europeans are immigrants to the Canary Islands.

◀ ◀ *Opposite: A wide variety of fruit is produced on Tenerife, but manyagricultural workers have left the land to work in the tourist industry.*
◀ *Left:* Tinerfeños *enjoy their weekends, when eating out is a popular pastime.*

INTRODUCING TENERIFE

VIRGIN DEL CARMEN FESTIVAL

The Virgin del Carmen is the patron saint of fishermen and seafarers. Each July the fishing villages around the coast of Tenerife celebrate this saint with a spectacular festival. The image of the Virgin is taken from the parish church and paraded around the streets, ending up at the beach or harbour. There she is taken briefly into the sea, either on the shoulders of the fishermen or on a boat, before being taken back to her sanctuary. The fiesta is accompanied by singing, dancing, fireworks and the cooking of giant paellas.

Religion

The Spanish conquerors brought **Roman Catholicism** with them to the Canary Islands and they swiftly converted the Guanches. It is still the official religion and it plays an important part in people's lives. Although weekly church attendance is not high, most *tinerfeños* have church baptisms, weddings and funerals and support religious feast days. There are a number of churches of other denominations, plus a mosque.

Festivals

Fiestas are the traditional way of celebrating saints' days on the religious calendar. These include *Candelaria*, the patron saint of the Canary Islands; *Corpus Christi*, when floral carpets are laid out on the streets; Easter, which usually involves statues of the Virgin being paraded through the streets; and *Nuestra Señora de la Luz* marked by processions of boats. **Romerias** are processions led by decorated ox carts which head from town churches to a hermitage or similar location. Other festivals are of a secular nature and may include week-long *ferias* or fairs. The *Carnaval* (Carnival) at Santa Cruz, which rivals that at Rio, is outstanding. Fiestas are usually accompanied by fireworks, bonfires, parades, traditional singing and folk dancing. Some festivals, such as the Rain Festival at Teide, are believed to date back to the times of the Guanches, while on other occasions old historical events are acted out.

▼ *Below: An old church in Puerto de la Cruz.*

Sport and Recreation

The Canary Islands have some unique forms of sport that go back centuries and are enthusiastically followed by the locals. **Lucha Canaria**, or Canarian Wrestling, probably had its origin in

Guanche trials of strength. Bullfighting is not popular in the Canary Islands, but sand covered arenas resembling bullrings are used for the wrestling competitions. The rules are strict. There are two teams of 12 participants or *luchadores*. Two contestants at a time attempt to throw each other to the ground in a best of

▲ *Above: El Médano, with its persistent winds, is the best windsurfing spot on the island.*

three competition or *brega*. Only the soles of the feet must touch the ground. Canarian wrestling is not a violent sport, as punching and kicking are not allowed. Skill and balance are more important than weight and size. The team which wins the most *bregas* claims the overall match. *Luchas* are often held at original Guanche locations and at fiestas. **Juego del Palo**, or stick fighting, also originated in pre-Conquest days. It is a contest using 2m (6.5ft) wooden staves called *banot*. Even longer staves of around 2.5m (8ft) are used in the **salto del pastor canario**, a form of pole vaulting in which contestants leap down the mountainside and across deep ravines. Less appealing to tourists will be **cock fighting**, which has a strong following in Tenerife.

The more international spectator sports are also hugely popular in the Canary Islands. As in the rest of Spain, **football** is obsessively followed. Club Deportivo Tenerife are in the Spanish Second Division and their local derbys against rivals UD Las Palmas are among the highlights of the sporting year. Other sports include beach volleyball, tennis and golf. There are many possibilities for **water sports**, both for locals and tourists. **Sailing**, **water-skiing**, **windsurfing** and **power-boat racing** are all highly popular. The clear, warm Atlantic is ideal for **scuba diving** and **snorkelling** and there are a number of underwater national parks around the island. The ocean also provides ideal conditions for **deep-sea fishing**. Charter boats are available to catch marlin, tunny, shark and swordfish.

WALKERS AND DOGS

Tenerife has some superb walking country, particularly in the **Anaga Mountains**, the **Teno Massif** and in the **Mount Teide National Park**. A common problem in the first two areas is the attention that walkers receive from dogs. In most cases their bark is worse than their bite, and even the more ferocious will be deterred by a walking stick or the action of picking up a stone. For particularly nervous hikers there are ultrasonic dog-scarers that can be used. A different sort of problem is the over-friendly dog who latches on to you and just will not go away!

INTRODUCING TENERIFE

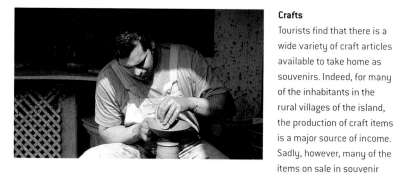

▲ Above: Traditional pottery-making has changed little since Guanche times.
▶ Opposite: Statue of poet-novelist Ángel Guimerá.

GUANCHE ARTISTIC SEALS

Although the Guanches had no knowledge of metals, the wheel or the bow and arrow, they were certainly not without artistic ability, particularly with regard to ceramics. They made pots with the coil method rather than using a wheel, and produced a wide range of other ceramic goods, including jewellery and small symbolic figurines (replicas of which can be bought in shops). The **Museo de la Naturaleza y el Hombre** in Santa Cruz has hundreds of examples of small ceramic discs that have been painted or etched with designs, usually of a geometric kind. They tend to be described as 'artistic seals', but their true purpose is debatable. Were they for personal ornamentation, a form of currency or for pressing into clay to conclude business? We may never know.

Crafts

Tourists find that there is a wide variety of craft articles available to take home as souvenirs. Indeed, for many of the inhabitants in the rural villages of the island, the production of craft items is a major source of income. Sadly, however, many of the items on sale in souvenir shops are cheap imitations from abroad and this is a major threat to the survival of ancient craft skills.

Many of the handicrafts that are so admired by tourists, were in fact essential to the daily agricultural way of life in past centuries. The **woodworking** skills can be seen on the ornately carved balconies of the older towns of Tenerife and on furniture and cedarwood chests. The main wood-carving centres are at La Laguna and La Orotava. **Basketwork**, using wood, cane, straw and palm leaves, is a common craft throughout the island. Examples include straw hats, fans, baskets and bags. The craft of **pottery** dates right back to Guanche times and it is still made in the traditional way without using a wheel. The pots vary in size from the large urns which were once used to store olive oil, down to small vases and ashtrays. Look out for the small Guanche-style figurines. Probably the most attractive souvenirs (and the lightest to carry home) are the **textiles**. Embroidered cloth is seen to advantage in the colourful national costumes that are worn at local festivals. Tablecloths, napkins and handkerchiefs are the most commonly displayed items, but these are also the craft goods that are brought in from abroad. Look for the genuine articles at the schools of embroidery, such as that at the Casa de los Balcones at La Orotava. Other interesting craft souvenirs are the rag dolls in national costume, musical instruments such as the local *timple*, items made from polished volcanic stone and lace-work made by the island's nuns.

The Arts

Although the Guanches left numerous examples of wall paintings in caves, it was some time before any notable Spanish **painters** emerged. Most of the 17th-, 18th- and 19th-century artists confined their work to religious topics and some of their paintings may be seen in the churches of the island. During the 20th century, the island's main Impressionist artist was Manuel González Méndez (1843–1909). Another well-known artist was Néstor de la Torre (1887–1938), who specialized in murals and was responsible for a campaign to revive Canarian folk art and architecture. The work of the versatile César Manrique (1919–1992), artist, architect and environmentalist, can be seen throughout the Canary Islands, particularly in the design of outdoor swimming complexes.

As far as **sculpture** is concerned, the name of José Luján Pérez (1756–1815) stands out. His work can be found in churches and cathedrals throughout the Canary Islands.

Although the Guanches had no written language, **literature** has a long history in the Canary Islands. Indeed there is a well-known saying 'the Canaries is a land of poets'. Certainly there have been many novelists and poets over the centuries, but most of them have had to move to the mainland to gain recognition. Some of the best-known are José de Viera y Clavijo (1731–1813), Benito Pérez Galdós (1843–1920) and Ángel Guimerá (1849–1924).

There are some fine museums and art galleries in the Canary Islands. On Tenerife, try to visit the Museo de la Naturaleza y el Hombre and the Museo Municipal de Bellas Artes in Santa Cruz. The former, located in the old city hospital, has a superb display of Guanche culture. The Casa de Carta ethnological museum displays a comprehensive collection of regional costumes.

GUANCHE SKULL PIERCING

In the Museo de la Naturaleza y El Hombre in Santa Cruz are around 1000 skulls dating back to Guanche times. Many of them show the drilled holes that were typical of the Guanches. In the medical world, the process is known as 'trepanning' and is carried out with metal drills. However, the Guanches had no knowledge of metals, so they must have carried out this custom with stone – probably the volcanic rock known as obsidian. Why did they carry out this gruesome practice? Was it to let evil spirits out? Was it done while they were living or after they died? The questions remain unanswered.

INTRODUCING TENERIFE

► *Opposite: A typical Canarian balcony like this one can be found in many of the older towns.*

Music and Dance

Although the Canary Islands have not produced any noted composers, classical music is taken seriously and the Tenerife Symphony Orchestra is well supported. The orchestra is now based at the Auditorio de Tenerife – a spectacular concert hall in Santa Cruz. Traditional folk music and dancing are always prominent in fiesta times. Dances include the lively *isa* and the more dignified *folia*. Occasionally the *tajaraste* may be performed. This dance is believed to have had its origins in Guanche times. The dancing is accompanied by traditional instruments such as castanets (*characas*) and the *timple* (*see* panel, this page). Many dances, such as the *malagueña* and the *sevillaña*, have been introduced by immigrants from Andalucía. Popular music, on the other hand, seems to have been influenced from the other direction, with dominant Latin American *salsa* rhythms.

Architecture

The Guanches, who were largely cave dwellers, left little legacy in the way of vernacular architecture. The oldest buildings in Tenerife, therefore, date back to the Spanish Conquest. Since this time, no destructive wars have occurred and this fact, combined with the mild weather, has meant that many of the island's ancient buildings are in a good state of preservation.

The Gothic style was going out of fashion at the time of the Conquest, with the result that many of the early buildings were constructed in the *Mudéjar* style, which had been bequeathed to the Spaniards by the Moors. In domestic design, the *Mudéjar* style encompasses the need for water and protection from the sun. Most houses are built around a central courtyard or patio, frequently with a decorated well. In the larger houses, the *patio* had shady trees and a colonnaded cloister. This scheme was also common on the front of the house, with a columned, covered walkway at ground level and a balcony at first floor level. The balconies were made of wood and often highly decorated. There are some superb examples of this colonial style in the old parts of La Laguna and La Orotava.

THE UNUSUAL *TIMPLE*

On the island of Tenerife, most traditional dancing and songs are accompanied by the *timple* (pronounced 'tim-play'). It is a wooden, stringed instrument closely akin to the ukelele and the mandolin. It is made of wood and has a rounded back. It normally has five strings, although there is a four-string version called the contra, which is found on Lanzarote. Once thought to have originated from the Spanish *guitarillo*, it is now believed to have been brought to the islands by Berber slaves. Whenever there is a local fiesta, the *timple* will be much in evidence. It was even exported to Latin American countries with the many waves of emigrants and it figures strongly in the folk music of Cuba and Venezuela. The souvenir shops at Tenerife airport sell CDs featuring *timple* music and they make a fitting momento of a holiday on the island.

Artisans' houses from the same period are much simpler stone and whitewashed buildings, which feature predominantly flat roofs in the drier south of the island and tiled roofs in the wetter parts.

There is a good way of dating houses in Tenerife – up to the end of the 17th century, windows were often placed irregularly but from the 17th century onwards, house frontages became symmetrical, with a central door and equal-sized windows. A number of other architectural styles can be seen in Tenerife. By the 16th century, the *Mudéjar* style had been replaced with the intricate **Plateresque**, named after the work of silversmiths and particularly evident in some of the carved ceilings. By the 19th century, **Portuguese Baroque** had appeared, typified by the ornate iron railings on balconies. During the same period, public buildings such as town halls and museums were being constructed in the **neoclassical** style. The early 20th century saw some interesting **Art Nouveau** buildings, mainly the work of César Manrique. The second half of the century saw the growth of tourism and with it some rather ugly multistorey apartment blocks. More recent tourist development is of the low-rise variety and much more sympathetic to the environment.

TENERIFE'S CHURCHES

Tenerife has only one cathedral, but it does have several marvellous churches. Many date from the early 16th century and display a variety of styles. Few are genuinely Gothic, but there are many in the *Mudéjar* style, from the Moorish occupation of southern Spain. Others display the ornate Plateresque decoration. Some have carved wooden ceilings. Stained-glass windows are generally uninspiring, but this is more than compensated for by superb interiors. Altar screens (*retablos*) are often highly carved and dripping with gold leaf. Many churches have wooden carvings by Luján Pérez (1756–1815), the greatest of the Canarian sculptors. Remember that beachwear is inappropriate in churches and not appreciated by the locals.

INTRODUCING TENERIFE

Food and Drink

The **food** of Tenerife illustrates a wide range of influences from other countries, including mainland Spain, northern Europe and even the Americas. Typically Canarian food is most likely to be found in the capital, Santa Cruz, and in the more rural areas, rather than in the main resorts where the restaurants tend to serve food of an international persuasion. The visitor must first adjust to the unusual meal times in Tenerife (outside the hotels). **Breakfast** (*desayuno*) is generally light and rarely provided before 09:30. It usually consists of coffee, a sandwich (*bocadillo*) or a small cake (*pastel*). **Lunch** (*almuerzo*) is taken late, rarely before 14:30 and may have been preceded by *tapas*, which are light snacks served at the bar. Lunch for many *tinerfeños* will be the main meal of the day. **Dinner** (*cena*) is a lighter meal for the locals, who would rarely think of eating before 20:00. Hotel meals, of course, keep to more international timing.

There are two items of Canarian food which should be sampled. The traditional island staple food, going back to Guanche times, is *gofio*, which is ground and toasted wheat or maize. Served with most main courses are *papas arugadas*, which are small new potatoes with wrinkly skins which have been boiled in very salty water.

Main meals usually begin with a 'starter' such as salad (*ensalada*) or soup (*sopa*). Particular favourites are fish soup (*sopa de pescado*) and vegetable soup (*sopa de verdura*). Most restaurants will also offer the mainland cold soup *gazpacho*, which consists of tomatoes, onions and garlic. The main course will usually involve meat (*carne*) or fish (*pescado*). The most commonly offered meats are beef

GOFIO

This is one of the few culinary items to have survived from Guanche times. *Gofio* was once made from the glasswort plant, but after the Spanish introduced Indian corn, or maize, this became the main ingredient. It is mixed with wheat flour and toasted (or roasted), and then used in a variety of ways. It can be sprinkled on food and can also be used to thicken stews or soups. *Gofio* can also be made into a breakfast food. Another use is to mix it with figs or almonds to make a sweet. However, few visitors to Tenerife will ever have the opportunity to try *gofio*, as it is rarely on the menu in the main tourist resorts. Those who are keen to try this Canarian staple food will need to drive into the interior and find a rural restaurant with *gofio* on the menu.

(*ternera*), chicken (*pollo*), lamb (*cordero*), pork (*cerdo*) and rabbit (*conejo*). The prolific wild rabbits are shot widely on the islands, but others are reared domestically for the table. The meat may be grilled (*a la parilla*), roasted (*asado*) or come in a stew (*estofado* or *puchero*). A mouth watering variety of **fish** and **shellfish** can be found on the menu. Fish is usually prepared simply, being fried or grilled (*a la plancha*). At some of the better fish restaurants, it is possible to choose your own fish from a tank or a cold cabinet. You then pay by weight. The most common fish on the menu are sea bass (*cherne*), hake (*merluza*), swordfish (*pez espada*), sole (*lenguado*), tuna (*atún* or *bonito*) and parrot fish (*vieja*). Some excellent shellfish can be found, including prawns (*gambas*) and mussels (*mejillones*). Squid (*calamares*) is also very popular. Particular Tenerife specialities are the sauces which are provided with both fish and meat dishes. The red *mojo rojo* is a spicy vinaigrette-type sauce made from a mixture of chilli, cumin, paprika and saffron, usually served with meat. *Mojo verde* is a green variation with coriander or parsley used instead of paprika, making a perfect accompaniment to fish. Vegetables are rather limited on the Tenerife menu and salad is usually served as a garnishing with most main dishes.

NIBBLES — SPANISH STYLE

Tapas are believed to have originated in Seville during the 19th century, when drinkers protected their glass of *fino* from dust, flies and dripping hams by putting a cover or tapa over their glass. The cover was often a slice of bread, on which enterprising bartenders began to add food. The rest, as they say, is history. Spain's quirky mealtimes encourage 'grazing' – taking the occasional snack to fill the gap. The days when a free *tapa* was provided with a drink are over, but a **tapas crawl** is one of the delights of Tenerife, particularly in the capital, Santa Cruz. *Tapas* vary from a simple dish of olives or a slice of cheese, to quite sophisticated dishes. Remember that it is cheaper to take your *tapas* standing at a bar, than sitting at a table.

◀ ◀ *Opposite:* Papas arugadas, *strongly salted new potatoes, accompany most main course dishes.*
◀ *Left: Squid –* calamares *or* pulpa *– can be prepared in a variety of ways.*

INTRODUCING TENERIFE

The choice of **desserts** (*postres*) is usually confined to traditional Spanish favourites such as crème caramel (*flan*), ice cream (*helado*) or fruit (*fruta*). Any local **cheese** on offer will be unusual, such as the Tenerife white goat's cheese (*queso blanco*). Another interesting speciality is *queso de flor*, which is a mixture of cow's and sheep's milk flavoured with the flowers of a thistle.

The main resort areas of Tenerife also offer a bewildering selection of foreign restaurants. Chinese and Indian restaurants are particularly common, but many other nationalities are represented. Visitors on a budget should try the menu of the day (*menu del dia*), which usually offers a starter, a main course and a sweet, plus a drink, for a bargain price.

Sampling **alcoholic drinks** is an essential part of many people's holiday and Tenerife offers plenty of choice, including some local specialities. The production of **wine** has a long history on the island, providing a considerable amount of Malmsey or Canary Sack to Elizabethan England. Made from the sweet Malvasia grape, there is still a small amount of Malmsey in production today, but Tenerife cannot compete

with Madeira for this type of wine. The quality of Tenerife's table wines has improved greatly in recent years, with red wines produced in the areas around Tacorante, Santa Ursula and La Victoria. White and rosé wines come from Icod de los Vinos and La Guancha, and some have gained *denominación de origen* status. Most of the Tenerife wines are produced for local consumption, so to satisfy the demands of hotels and restaurants, a large amount of wine is imported from mainland Spain. There are some popular wine-based summer drinks including *tinto de verano*, a mixture of red wine and lemonade, and the deceptively strong *sangria*, which is a combination of red wine, liqueurs and lemonade garnished with ice and fruit. The local **beer** in Tenerife is the very drinkable *Dorada*, which is sold in bottled and draught form. For a small draught beer ask for *una caña*. A full range of foreign beers is also available. Amongst the **spirits** are some popular mainland brandies (*coñac*) such as *Soberano* and *Fundador*. The best known local spirit is rum (*ron*), which is made from sugar cane. Another variety is *ron miel*, a rum liqueur with added honey. There are a number of other **liqueurs**, many of which are made from the subtropical fruits grown on Tenerife. The most popular is *cobana*, a yellow banana liqueur that comes in a striking bottle. Remember that measures of spirits are two or three times more than one would expect at home!

The most popular of the **non-alcoholic drinks** is coffee, which comes in a variety of forms. Any bar with a reputation will make their coffee in an 'espresso' machine and for an espresso-type coffee ask for either a *café solo* (which is black) or a *café cortado* (which has just a touch of milk). *Café con leche* is a milky coffee. Don't be surprised to find that your coffee arrives in a glass. *Canarios* often take a shot of rum in their coffee or have an accompanying *coñac*. Tea is also available, but is usually served rather weak. Chocolate is a popular breakfast drink for *tinerfeños* and is usually consumed with *churros* (a form of doughnut). There is a full range of soft drinks (*refrescos*) and fruit juices (*zumos*).

BUSY BEES

Tenerife's bees produce one of its most popular souvenirs – honey. They forage the hillsides pollinating the numerous species of wild flowers and aromatic plants and in turn impart these particular flavours to the finished products. Speciality honeys include those flavoured by *tajinaste* – the Tenerife bugloss – a flowering plant of the family *Boraginaceae*, and *retama*, a broom of the family *Fabaceae*.

◀ *Opposite: Local wines rarely reach hotels and supermarkets, which prefer varieties from the mainland.*

2
Santa Cruz de Tenerife

Santa Cruz de Tenerife – more widely known as just Santa Cruz – is the capital of both Tenerife and the western province of the Canary Islands, which includes the islands of La Gomera, La Palma and El Hierro. It is a bustling modern city with nearly a quarter of a million inhabitants (one third of the island's inhabitants), covering an area of 150km² (58 sq miles). The suburbs spread north to the Anaga Mountains and southwest towards the Cumbre Dorsal. Santa Cruz shares the government of the Canary Islands with Las Palmas (on Gran Canaria). It is one of the largest ports in Spain, benefiting historically from transatlantic trade. The port has adapted to modern times and today the emphasis is on containers, ferries and cruise liners.

The city has a long history, going back to the arrival of the **Conquistadors** in 1494. Although many of Santa Cruz's historic buildings have been lost to modern development, sufficient remain to create a pleasant atmosphere in the central area of the city. However, only a small minority of the tourists who come to Tenerife visit Santa Cruz. This is a pity as the city makes an interesting day trip, with its seafront promenade, leafy squares, historic churches and excellent museums. Some tour operators run coach trips to Santa Cruz for the express purpose of shopping. Since Santa Cruz became a 'free port' in 1852 it has been able to sell its goods duty free, offering many shopping bargains. For the independent traveller there is much more to see than shops. From the central square, the Plaza de España, the sights of interest are within easy walking distance.

TOP ATTRACTIONS

*** Museo de la Naturaleza y el Hombre: information on the way of life of the ancient Guanches.
** Iglesia de Nuestra Señora de la Concepción: a church with an octagonal tower and a lovely interior.
* Mercado de Nuestra Señora de Africa: Santa Cruz's busy market.
* Parque Municipal García Sanabria: a shady park and gardens – a peaceful break from the bustle of the city.
* Parque Marítimo: César Manrique's beautifully designed sea-water lido built on derelict dockland.

◄ *Opposite: View over Santa Cruz and the harbour.*

SANTA CRUZ DE TENERIFE

Santa Cruz de Tenerife

For more information regarding **rainfall** and **temperatures** in Santa Cruz, see page 45.

CLIMATE

Santa Cruz is in the cloudier and wetter north of the island, but its coastal position in the rain shadow of the Anaga Mountains, means that it often escapes the cloud and rain that is found inland at higher altitude. For more information regarding **rainfall** and **temperatures** in Santa Cruz, see page 45.

A recent development has been the increasing number of cruise ships that call at Santa Cruz, which has had to adapt to this new form of tourism.

THE HISTORY OF SANTA CRUZ

Santa Cruz's history really began on 3 May 1494, when **Alonso Fernández de Lugo** landed on the beach which the Guanches called Añaza. De Lugo planted his Holy Cross on the beach and it was from this cross that the city acquired its name. A fortress was quickly built to defend the settlement and de Lugo set about subduing the Guanches, a task which was to take many years. Santa Cruz was slow to grow. La Laguna was the first capital of the island and Garachico, on the north of the island and facing the New World, became the chief port. However, Garachico was largely destroyed by a volcanic eruption in 1706 and business moved to Santa Cruz. By the 18th and 19th centuries, aided by the slave trade and transatlantic commerce, the port of Santa Cruz was flourishing, and in 1723 it replaced La Laguna as the island's capital.

With the success of the port came new perils as it became the target of rival seafarers and pirates. Attacks came from Berbers, the Dutch and French Huguenots, but Santa Cruz's main problems came from English 'sea dogs' such as Drake, Hawkins and Blake. The most famous incident concerned the attack on Santa Cruz in 1797 by **Admiral Horatio Nelson**, who was ordered to raid the port and capture two ships loaded with bullion from Manila. Nelson's attack was a spectacular failure, as the defenders of the port had been forewarned of his supposedly surprise assault. In addition, rough seas scattered his flotilla of small landing boats. Many of Nelson's men were drowned, killed or wounded and the Admiral himself lost an arm in the battle. However, the victors were magnanimous and after treating Nelson's wounded sailors in the local hospital, they were returned to their ships with various gifts. The Admiral is said to have sent back English cheese and a

▼ *Below: This craft shop in Santa Cruz also sells local costumes.*

SANTA CRUZ DE TENERIFE

PLAY IT SAFE

Tenerife has relatively low levels of crime, but it would be foolish not to acknowledge the fact that street crime does occur here. Most visitors will be perfectly safe, but a few simple precautions will lessen the risks. Do not carry credit cards or large amounts of cash around with you. Keep cash in a belt or pouch rather than in your pockets. Take care with cameras, especially when sitting at café tables. Beware of pickpockets when on crowded buses or at street markets. Keep to well lit streets at night. Make sure that your car is locked and that no valuables are left in sight. Should you be the victim of a street crime, ring the police on **091**.

keg of beer – which was a civilized ending to the fiasco. This was to be Nelson's only defeat in his glorious career.

In 1852, Queen Isabella II of Spain made Tenerife a **free trade zone** and Santa Cruz became a free port, which brought more prosperity to the city. However, as most goods produced on Tenerife were exported through Santa Cruz, the port's trade reflected the island's 'boom and bust' economy as the monoculture in sugar cane, cochineal and bananas went through their cycles. The growth of tourism in the second half of the 20th century has only indirectly affected Santa Cruz, but the city has a busy, prosperous air and its port continues to thrive.

THE HISTORIC CENTRE OF SANTA CRUZ
Plaza de España ★★★

The centrepiece of Santa Cruz and an excellent place to start a walking tour of the city is the **Plaza de España**. It was laid out in the 1940s on the site of the old San Cristobel castle. Important events have always taken place in the square and in 1987, during the *Carnaval*, Plaza de España claimed a place in the Guinness Book of Records, when over 200,000 people attended an outdoor dance here. The Plaza de España has several links with the Fascist era and dominating the area is the cruciform **Monumento a los Caídos** – the Monument to the Fallen in the Spanish Civil War (1936–39). There is a small memorial chapel at the base of the monument, from where a lift leads to the top, giving good views over the city and the harbour. Sadly, both the chapel and the lift are usually closed. The square has undergone a major refurbishment in recent years, with the scene graced with a large pond backed with some curious huts made of black volcanic material

▼ *Below: The plant-roofed Tourist Information Centre in Plaza de España.*

topped with soil, on which grows indigenous plants and flowers. One of these huts houses the new **Tourist Information Centre**, which can supply maps, brochures and accommodation details. Around the Plaza de España are a number of impressive public buildings. The one nearest the harbour is the **Palacio Insular** (or Cabildo), identified by its clock tower. The building mostly houses the offices of the island government. The foyer contains an interesting scale model of the island. The nearby building is the **Correos** or post office. Numerous cafés line the north side of the plaza, their tables spilling out onto the pavement.

▲ *Above: Fine buildings and quality shops are to be found in the tree-lined Plaza de la Candelaria.*

Plaza de la Candelaria ★★★

Leading off the Plaza de España is the much more attractive rectangular Plaza de la Candelaria. At the heart of the square is the Triunfo de la Candelaria, a monument in Carrera marble, carved by a Genoese sculptor. Topping it is a statue of the **Madonna de la Candelaria**, the patron saint of the islands. She carries, traditionally, a candle in her left hand and a baby in her right hand. Supporting the narrow obelisk are four Guanche chiefs, symbolically converted to Christianity. Amongst the fine buildings around the square are the Palacio de Carta which dates from 1752 with an exceptional façade that melds neo-classical elements with Baroque features and the Casino de Tenerife, with its elaborate modernist elements.

THE PALACIO DE CARTA

At a time when major building works were usually undertaken by the church or the state, the Palacio de Carta is a major exception. Commissioned by Matias Rodriquez Carta as a family home, it remains one of the few civil buildings from this era on the island and was given protected status in 1947. Behind the sober façade lie a series of delightful patios, courtyards and balconies, but the building is currently not open to the public.

SANTA CRUZ DE TENERIFE

OTHER ATTRACTIVE SQUARES

Leading from the Plaza de la Candelaria is the pedestrianized Calle de Castillo, which is a shopper's delight, full of stores and bazaars. This road leads to the **Plaza de General Weyler**, with its marble fountain, trees and sculptures. Along one side is the neoclassical building of the **Capitanía General**, erected by General Valeirano Weyler towards the end of the 19th century. The square suffers badly from traffic noise, so for a more peaceful spot turn right along Avenida del 25 de Julio and after 300m (328yd) the **Plaza de la Patos** is reached. In the centre of this attractive square is a tiled fountain notable for its large statues of green frogs squirting water towards an elegant swan. Around the fountain are a series of seats also composed of tiles, which were made in the famous Santa Ana factory in Seville. The plaza is lined with modernist buildings, mainly used for government offices. Further to the east is the leafy **Plaza del Principe**, with a bandstand at its centre as well as numerous statues. Alongside the square, and approached via Calle Murphy, is the **Museo Municipal de Bellas Artes**, or Fine Arts Museum (open Tuesday–Friday, 10:00–20:00, Saturday–Sunday 10:00–15:00). It mainly displays the paintings and sculptures of local artists, but also occasionally has special exhibitions. Adjacent to the Fine Arts Museum, and entered from the opposite side of the block, is the **Iglesia de San Juzgados Francisco**, which is said to have been founded by Irish monks fleeing from persecution in Elizabethan England. The present church, which is distinguished by several *retablos* dripping with gold leaf, was once the chapel of a Franciscan friary.

NORTH OF THE CITY CENTRE
Parque Municipal García Sanabria ★★★

To escape from the bustle of the city, head for the **Parque Municipal García Sanabria**, located between the Rambla del General Franco and the Calle Méndez Nuñez. The park also operates as botanical gardens and is full of fountains, trees and promenades. It is notable for its fine collection of statues left over from the International Exhibition of Street Sculpture in 1973. More sculptures can be seen along the Rambla, including Henry Moore's *The Warrior*.

Museo Militar de Almeyda ★★★

Where the Rambla meets the coastal Avenida de Anaga, you will see the **Museo Militar de Almeyda** (open Tuesday– Saturday, 10:00–14:00; free admission). This military museum is located in a 19th-century barracks. There are

◄◄ *Opposite: The well-kept Parque García Sanabria, notable for its collection of plants and statues.*
◄ *Left: The plain exterior of the Museo Militar conceals some fascinating displays.*

SANTA CRUZ DE TENERIFE

A MODERN TRANSPORT LINK

The chronic parking system in Santa Cruz has been eased by the opening in 2007 of a modern **tram service** linking the city with the university town of La Laguna. The colourful trams largely run on some old rails which were last used in 1957 and the service has proved to be hugely popular with commuters who no longer have the problem of where to park their cars. The tram terminal is close to the Auditorio. For details of prices and timings, visit www. metrotenerife.com

two main aspects to the museum. The first concerns General Franco, who spent four months in Tenerife as Commander General before leaving to conduct the Spanish Civil War. The other section inevitably deals with Nelson's botched attack on Santa Cruz in 1797. You can see the cannon called El Tigre (the tiger), which is supposed to have fired the shot that hit Nelson's right arm, which was later amputated. Before leaving the area, seek out the superb fountain in the museum's grounds.

SOUTH OF THE CITY CENTRE

Three blocks southwest of the Plaza de España is the **Teatro Guimerá**, which is the home of the Tenerife Symphony Orchestra and used for theatre, opera and ballet performances. It was named after the dramatist Angel Guimerá, who, although born in Santa Cruz, did most of his work in Catalonia. The theatre, which dates from 1849, was built on the site of an old Dominican convent. Outside, there is an unusual statue in the form of a theatrical mask, which gives

some curious optical effects.

Also to the south of the city centre, and close to the bus station and the sea shore, is the **Parque Marítimo** (tel: 922 22 93 68). This is a successful example of urban renewal in what was once a derelict dock area. The complex centres around the old **Castillo de San Juan** (Castle of St John) and consists of a large sea water lido designed by the late César Manrique, the famous architect and environmentalist from Lanzarote. There are future plans for a maritime museum and other leisure facilities. Unfortunately, the nearby oil refinery spoils

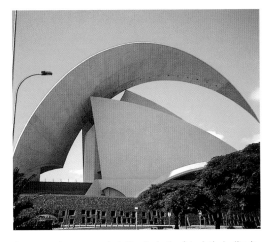

◀ *Left: The futuristic Auditorio, a concert hall shaped like a wave.*
◀◀ *Opposite: The bell tower of the Iglesia de Nuestra Señora de la Concepción rises above the city roofs.*

the atmosphere somewhat. Nearby is the futuristic Auditorio (*see* panel, this page) and on the other side of the road, the modern Conference Centre, backed by the El Corte Inglés department store.

Iglesia de Nuestra Señora de la Concepción ★★★
Approaching the dry river bed of the **Barranco de los Santos**, the six-tiered Moorish-looking tower of the **Iglesia de Nuestra Señora de la Concepción** comes into view. The octagonal turret on the top was used as a lookout point if pirates were expected. The original building was founded in 1502 by the Conquistadors, but it was badly damaged by fire in 1652 and underwent considerable restoration in the 17th and 18th centuries. There was further restoration in the 1990s and the church is now open. Apart from the tower, the exterior does not resemble a church at all and the visitor has to struggle to find the main entrance (look for the traditional wooden Canarian balconies). The interior, however, is a gem. There are sturdy pillars of contrasting volcanic stone and a panelled Portuguese ceiling. There are the traditional five naves (the main nave and four large aisles) and ornately carved Canary wood choir stalls. Above the High Altar is the figure of the Mater Doloroso carved by Luján Pérez. To the left of the

A NEW LANDMARK

In the autumn of 2003 a startling new building was opened close to the Parque Marítimo on Santa Cruz's seafront. This is the **Auditorio de Tenerife**, a concert hall designed like a wave, and as distinctive a building as Sydney's Opera House. It was the work of the architect Santiago Calatrava, who also designed the airport in Bilbao, the train station in Lyon and the museum in Milwaukee. The Auditorio cost €75 million (£51 million) and most people in Tenerife consider the money well spent. It is the home of the prestigious Tenerife Symphony Orchestra and there is a full programme of opera, jazz, symphonic and chamber music for locals and tourists to enjoy. www.auditoriodetenerife.com

SANTA CRUZ DE TENERIFE

▶ *Right: Part of the curious collection of Guanche skulls in the Museo de la Naturaleza y el Hombre.*
▶▶ *Opposite: Cars line up for the busy ferry in the port of Santa Cruz.*

THE CHANGING PORT

The port of Santa Cruz has been one of the busiest in Spain since the mid-1600s. Throughout its history it has been forced to adapt to changing trade demands and conditions. For centuries it was a staging post for goods, ships and passengers crossing the Atlantic, and had an important role in exporting the island's agricultural commodities such as bananas and sugar cane. Today, most goods are transported in containers. This has led to the growth of a large area of container docks alongside the coast road to the northeast of the port, marked by huge straddle carriers and other handling equipment. The port also provides facilities for a number of ferry boats, both from mainland Spain and from neighbouring islands. Large oil tankers from all over the world bring crude oil to the refinery south of the port. In recent years the biggest growth area in shipping has been with cruise liners, and Tenerife has proved a popular port of call for these vessels. There is easy walking access from the cruise terminal to the town centre.

altar is the Chapel of the Holy Heart, which contains the Holy Cross carried by Alonso Fernández de Lugo when he first set foot on the island and which gave the city its name. To the right of the altar is the Carta Chapel. Note the *retablo*, which was carved on the order of Don Matías Carta. He died before it was completed and the skull and crossbones on the floor marks his tomb. His portrait is on the west wall of the chapel. It was painted after his death, as shown by the closed eyes and crossed arms. The church originally contained the English banners captured during Nelson's abortive raid, but these were transferred to the Military Museum during the recent renovations and are unlikely to be returned.

Museo de la Naturaleza y el Hombre ★★★

Opposite the church on the other side of the Barranco de Santos, is the excellent **Museo de la Naturaleza y el Hombre** – the Museum of Nature and Man (Tuesday–Saturday 09:00–20:00, Sunday–Monday , 10:00–17:00; admission charge, free on Friday– Saturday 16:00–20:00). The museum was opened in 1997 in the old city hospital building. There is an excellent section on the flora and fauna of Tenerife, but most visitors will want to see the extensive archaeological section on the customs and art of the Guanches. There are over 1000 skulls on display, some showing the curious drilled holes for which the Guanches were well known. There are also two mummies, one male and one female, and there is information on the mummification process. Not to be missed!

Mercado de Nuestra Señora de Africa ★★★

A stone's throw from the museum is the city market, the **Mercado de Nuestra Señora de Africa**. Entry is through a large arch flanked by numerous flower stalls. Further in is a colourful collection of stalls selling fish, meat, fruit and vegetables, giving a genuine flavour of Tenerife life. On Sunday mornings there is a busy flea market in the surrounding streets.

MUMMIFICATION

One of the highlights of a visit to the Museo de la Naturaleza y el Hombre is the opportunity to see Guanche **mummies**. The Guanches mummified corpses in a similar but cruder way to the ancient Egyptians. It appears that only the higher echelons of society were treated in this way. Intestines were removed from the bodies, which were then soaked in goats' milk and wrapped with reeds and animal skins. The bodies were then left in the sun to dry for around 14 days. This unpleasant work was carried out by lower-caste Guanches, who tended to be ostracized by society. The bodies were placed in remote, inaccessible caves, and for this reason mummies are still being found today. It also appears that the mummified chiefs or menceyes were laid in wooden boxes which were then placed upright against the cave walls.

SANTA CRUZ DE TENERIFE AT A GLANCE

Best Time to Visit

Although Santa Cruz is located in the wetter north of the island, its coastal position means that it misses much of the cloud and rain that is found at some of the higher levels. From a climatic point of view, therefore, any time of the year is suitable for a visit to the capital. It does get extremely hot in summer, which some people might find rather trying, but there are plenty of shady outdoor cafés to recharge the batteries.

Getting There

Public service buses, which are operated by the TITSA company (tel: 922 53 13 00, website: www.titsa.com) run a variety of routes to Santa Cruz from all parts of the island: 101 from Puerto de la Cruz, 110 (express service) and 111 from Costa Adeje/Los Cristianos, 343 from Los Cristianos (via the North Airport) and 112 from the Costa del Silencio. There are a number of regular shuttle buses that travel from both the airports. There are also tour groups that run **coach** excursions from all of the main resorts to Santa Cruz. Try Top Excursions, tel: 922 71 90 50; www.topexcursionstravel.com Visitors who have **hire cars** will easily be able to reach the city from most of the main resorts within an hour's journey using the motorways.

Getting Around

Most of the main sights and attractions of Santa Cruz are within easy walking distance of the Plaza de España and are usually best visited on foot. **Taxis**, however, are cheap and plentiful, with a convenient taxi rank located right in the Plaza de España. A **tram** service, started in 2007, links Santa Cruz with La Laguna. It follows part of the track of an old street car system which closed down in 1951. It is popular with commuters and students, while it can be useful for tourists as it stops at a number interesting locations. It is the only tram or train operating in the Canary Islands. For details of routes and fares visit www.metrotenerife.com

Where to Stay

Santa Cruz is not primarily a holiday resort, so its hotels are mainly for business people.

Luxury
Iberostar Grand Hotel Mencey, Calle José Naveiras 38, tel: 922 60 90 00, fax: 922 28 60 17, www.grandhotelmencey.com This is the city's top hotel, luxuriously appointed and frequented by royalty, who no doubt appreciate the opulence of its Louis XIV style of furnishings. Casino in the basement.

Mid-range
Atlantico, Calle de Castillo 12, tel: 922 24 63 75, fax: 922 24 63 78, www.hotelatlanticotenerife.com A modern hotel, situated in a relatively quiet but convenient part of the city.
Taburiente, Calle José Naveiras 24A, tel: 922 27 60 00, fax: 922 27 05 62, www.hoteltaburiente.com This well-appointed hotel is close to the municipal park. It has a swimming pool.
Barcelo Santa Cruz Contemporáneo, Rambla del General Franco 116, tel: 922 27 15 71, fax: 922 27 12 23, www.barcelo.com Bargain prices in a pleasant part of the city.

Budget
Horizonte, Calle Santa Rosa de Lima 11, tel: 922 27 19 36, www.horizontetenerife.com This is a small, friendly and well-placed little hotel.
Tanausu, Calle Padre Anchieta 8, tel: 922 21 70 00, fax: 922 21 60 29, www.hoteltanausu.es A small hotel in the south of Santa Cruz. No restaurant.

Where to Eat

Bear in mind that the restaurants in Santa Cruz cater mainly for the inhabitants of the capital and therefore the atmosphere and dress tend to be more restrained than in the resorts. There are some excellent snack bars with outside tables in the Plaza de la Candelaria and along the Rambla del General Franco.

Luxury

El Coto de Antonio, Calle General Goded 13, tel: 922 27 21 05. Just off the Rambla and popular with the local business community.
Anocheza, Calle Santa Teresita 3, tel: 922 29 16 73, www. restoranteanocheza.com Excellent classical dishes with modern flair by one of the island's top chefs.
Solana, Calle Pérez de Rozas, tel: 922 24 37 80. A family run restaurant serving contemporary fine food.

Mid-range

Mesón Los Monjes, Paseo Milicias de Garachico 7, tel: 922 24 65 76. Centrally placed near the Plaza de España. Castilian decoration and recipes.

Budget

Many bars serve *tapas* or have a small dining room attached. Try one of these:
Guanchinche de Peter, Calle de la Noria; **Bar Mercado**, Calle de José Manuel Guimerá, next to the Sunday flea market. Other *tapas* bars can be found beside the Parque García Sanabria on Calle Dr José Navieras, including **Tasca de Enfrente** and **Tasca Tagoror**. For eating on the move try the delicious ice-cream from Il Gelato del Mercato in Mercato

Municipal Nuestra Senora de Africa.

TOURS AND EXCURSIONS

Few excursions actually run from Santa Cruz as hardly any tourists stay in the city itself. However, there are a number of sights around Santa Cruz that are on the itinerary of many of the tour companies. These include: the historic town of **La Laguna**, the **Museo de la Ciencia y el Cosmos** in La Laguna, the **Basilica** at **Candelaria**, and the **Ethnographic Museum** and **Pyramids** at **Güimar**.

USEFUL CONTACTS

Tourist Information Centre: Plaza de España, tel: 922 23 98 11; open Oct–Jun Mon–Fri, 08:00–18:00; Sat 09:00–13:00; Jul–Sep Mon–Fri, 08:00–17:00; Sat, 09:00–12:00. English-speaking staff, plenty of brochures available. There are also some 'tourist kiosks' scattered around the town.
Airports: Los Rodeos Airport (Tenerife Norte). For information, tel: 902 40 47 04; for bookings, contact individual airlines. Inter-island flights mainly leave from Los Rodeos. Contact **Binter Canarias** (tel: 902 39 13 92,

www.bintercanarias.com).
Reina Sofía Airport (Tenerife Sur). For information, tel: 902 40 47 04.
Ferries: The **Fred Olsen Line** (www.fredolsen.es) runs four ferries a day from Santa Cruz to Gran Canaria. Ferries run by **Trasmediterránea** (www. transmediterranea.es) leave once a week for Cádiz in mainland Spain, calling at Gran Canaria en route. Tickets for these ferries can be bought either at the Estación Marítima Muelle de Ribera on the quayside or from travel agents.
Hospitals: Hospital Universitario Nuestra Senora de Candelaria, Carettera General del Rosario 145, Santa Cruz; tel: 922 60 20 00.
Post Office: Plaza d'Espana, tel: 922 53 36 29; open Mon–Fri, 08:30–20:30; Sat, 09:30–13:00.
Consulates:
British Consulate: Plaza Weyler 8 (on the first floor), tel: 922 28 99 03; open Mon, Tue, Fri, 08:30–13:30.
Irish Consulate: Calle San Francisco 9, Santa Cruz, tel: 922 24 56 71. The nearest **US Consulate** is on neighbouring Gran Canaria.
Edificio ARCA, Calle Los Martinez Escobar 3, Las Palmas; tel: 928 27 12 59.

SANTA CRUZ	J	F	M	A	M	J	J	A	S	O	N	D
AVERAGE TEMP. °F	70	70	72	73	75	79	82	84	82	79	73	72
AVERAGE TEMP. °C	21	22	22	23	24	26	28	29	28	26	23	22
RAINFALL in	1.46	1.39	0.96	0.60	0.15	0.5	0	0.02	0.33	0.73	1.53	2
RAINFALL mm	37.3	35.5	24.3	15.2	3.8	1.3	0	0.6	8.5	18.5	38.9	51.0

3
Northeast Tenerife

The peninsula in the northeast of Tenerife is geologically speaking the oldest part of the island. Although the rocks were formed from the lava flows of a volcano, the area has no evidence of recent volcanic activity. The area is dominated by the **Anaga Mountains** which are composed of basalt. Their jagged peaks rise to just over 1000m (3300ft) and their lower slopes are clothed with laurel, pine trees and tree heather. This is also one of the wettest parts of Tenerife as the mountains are in the path of the rain-bearing **trade winds**. The cloud can be persistent, so visitors are advised to wait for a clear day before coming to the area. The Anaga Mountains are popular with walkers and numerous waymarked paths, which have survived since Guanche times, lead to remote villages such as **Chinamada** and **Hamorga**, where people still choose to live in cave houses. The marvellous scenery can be appreciated from a number of **miradors**, or lookouts, which are to be found at intervals along the road that runs along the spine of the range.

The gateway to the Anaga Mountains is the ancient city of **La Laguna**. Once the capital of Tenerife, it is an ecclesiastic centre with the island's only cathedral and a number of monasteries and convents. La Laguna is also the home of the only traditional university in the Canary Islands. Despite its attractions, the city sees few visitors and is largely ignored by tour operators and coach firms.

The eastern and western coasts present striking contrasts. On the more arid east coast the main attraction is the artificial beach of **Playa de las Teresitas**, the golden sand of

DON'T MISS

*** **Historic La Laguna:** full of mansions, palaces, churches and convents.
** **The Anaga Mountains:** jagged, forested mountains with good viewpoints.
** **Playa de las Teresitas**: a golden beach composed of sand brought from the Sahara Desert.
** **Casa de Carta:** the finest ethnographic museum in the Canary Islands.
** **Casa del Vino** *La Baranda*: popular wine museum and restaurant.

◀ *Opposite: The artificial Teresitas beach, with the village of San Andrés in the background.*

47

which was transported from the Sahara Desert. The western coast is lower lying and fertile, making it good farming country. Grapes grow particularly well in the area around **Tacoronte**. Don't miss the **Casa del Vino** *La Baranda*, a wine museum just outside the town. Near to Tacoronte is the pretty village of **El Sauzal**. Its white-domed church is one of the most photographed sights on the island.

The northwest coast also has a number of small holiday resorts, including **Mesa del Mar**. Further to the north are some larger resorts, such as **Bajamar** and **Punta del Hidalgo**, which are both popular with German visitors. This stretch of coast is mountainous and rocky, with rough seas, which means that swimming is safer in hotel pools.

San Andrés and Playa de las Teresitas ★★

The road northeast out of Santa Cruz passes along several kilometres of docks with towering container handling equipment, the Club Nautico and the increasingly common cruise liners, before reaching the attractive fishing village of **San Andrés**. Here the white houses straggle up the hillside, interspersed with pretty squares. Down at sea level, a number of excellent fish restaurants line the main road. A ruined fort can be seen on the northeastern outskirts of the village. It was constructed in the 18th century by Captain General Agustín de Robles. Just to the north, a crescent of golden sand marks the **Playa de las Teresitas**, a popular weekend venue for the inhabitants of Santa Cruz. Tenerife has few good beaches – they are mainly composed of boulders or black volcanic sand – but Playa de las Teresitas is undoubtedly the best. The beach, however, is entirely artificial – it is made up of over 4 million sacks of sand that were shipped in from the Sahara in the mid-1970s. A man-made stone reef protects the beach from storm waves and ensures safe swimming. The 2km (1-mile) long beach has plenty of facilities, including shady palm trees, beach bars, pedaloes and a windsurfing school. The land behind the beach has so far resisted development, but it's difficult to see that remaining the case in the long-term, and the authorities receive regular proposals for projects from local, national and international groups. The coast road continues as far as the picturesque village of Igueste. Halfway along the road is the quiet beach of **Playa de las Gaviotas**, which is popular with nudists. The road winds its way up to the Punta de los Organos, where a mirador gives stunning views all along the coast as far as Candelaria.

HEADING INLAND

The road from San Andrés into the interior leaves the arid coastline and heads into the mountains with a series of hairpin bends which are, nevertheless, well surfaced and engineered. The vegetation is more luxuriant and the laurel and pine forests hold declining populations of the endangered Bolle's and white-tailed laurel pigeons.

ENDANGERED PIGEONS

The laurel forests of the Anaga Mountains are home to two members of the pigeon family that are on the list of endangered species. They are the **Bolles laurel pigeon** and the **white-tailed laurel pigeon**. They are found only on Tenerife and the smaller islands of La Palma, El Hierro and La Gomera. The pigeons feed largely on laurel berries and lay only one egg in a nest in the lush vegetation that the laurel trees supply. Over the last two centuries the laurel forests have disappeared at an alarming rate to make way for agriculture, depriving the pigeons of their vital habitat.

◄ *Left: Playa de las Teresitas is composed of artificial sand brought from the Sahara Desert.*

▼ *Below: The remains of cave houses are common in the Anaga Mountains.*

El Bailadero ★★★

At the spine of the mountains the hamlet of **El Bailadero** is reached. The name comes from an old Guanche word, *baladero*, meaning 'bleating place'. It was here that the Guanches would bring their sheep in the hope that their bleating would persuade the gods to bring rain.

From El Bailadero there is a choice of routes. To the right a rough road leads to the remote hamlet of **Hamorga**, from whence footpaths lead down through the tiny settlement of Casas Blancas to the sea and Tenerife's most northerly lighthouse, the Faro de Anaga. The second route from El Bailadero runs northwards through a tunnel and then drops down along more hairpin bends to the white village of **Taganana**, which dates back to the early 16th century. It is worth stopping to look at the village church of Nuestra Señora de las Nieves (Our Lady of the Snows), one of the oldest on the island. If you can gain entry, don't miss the superb Flemish triptych, believed to date from the early 1500s. Taganana was once an important centre for the production of sugar and it is still a thriving agricultural centre with crops grown on its terraced hill slopes. The road continues along the shore to the small, rocky beaches of **San Roque**, **Almaciga** and **Benijo**, notable for their contorted rocks and sea caves.

The road soon peters out, but a footpath continues around the headland to the lighthouse.

Back at El Bailadero, the main route runs westwards along the spine of the mountains, with a series of miradors giving marvellous views in all directions. The first, a half mile from the main road, is the **Mirador Pico del Inglés**, said to be named after an

▲ *Above: A house is the subject of this charming wall decoration in La Laguna.*

Englishman who walked all the way here from La Laguna in a day. The views can be stupendous and on a clear day it is possible to see Mount Teide and even Gran Canaria. A rough road leads from the mirador to the remote village of **Las Carboneras**. From here, tracks can be followed to the hamlet of **Chinamada**, where the 30 or so inhabitants still live in **cave houses**. If you can look inside one of them you will find, however, that the interiors are far removed from the Stone Age (*see* panel, page 55). From the Mirador Pico del Inglés, the road continues west to **Las Mercedes**, where you find the **Mirador Cruz del Carmen**. Here there is a Visitors' Centre, picnic area and a busy restaurant. A viewing platform looks down over the dense laurel forest. There is also a small chapel containing the statue of Nuestra Señora de los Mercedes. Lastly, there is the **Mirador Jardín**, which gives fine views westward over La Laguna and across the Aguere valley towards Mount Teide.

La Laguna ✱✱✱

The city of **San Cristóbal de la Laguna** is the oldest settlement on the island of Tenerife. It was founded by Alfonso Fernández de Lugo after he had conquered the island in 1496, having defeated the Guanches at this spot. It remained the capital until it was superceded by Santa Cruz in 1723. La Laguna lies in a broad valley some 550m (1800ft) above sea level, where the climate is cooler than on the coast. It gains its name from a small lagoon that was drained in 1837, filled

CIGAR-MAKING CITY

The fact that many of the inhabitants of Tenerife have emigrated to Cuba and later returned may explain why the manufacture of cigars takes place in a number of towns on the island. The warm, sub-tropical climate, suits the cultivation of the tobacco plant, particularly near La Laguna, where there is an important cigar-making industry. The city is especially known for the hand made palmero, rolled within an individual leaf.

in and built over. Today, La Laguna is a city of contrasts. To the north of the commercial and shopping centre is the old part of the city – the *casco histórico*, largely responsible for the decision in 1999 to include La Laguna on UNESCO's World Heritage List. This area retains its original street plan laid out in a grid system. It is full of historical stone buildings, with wooden balconies and flower-filled patios. The old city's ecclesiastical importance is shown by its cathedral and a wealth of churches, monasteries and convents. To the south of the town centre you will find the modern university area, with the associated Astrophysics Institute and Museum of Science and Technology. Strangely, La Laguna sees relatively few tourists – a situation with which the local authorities seem quite happy. However, La Laguna can easily be reached via the motorway system and the historical quarter is one of the gems of the island.

PADRE ANCHIETA

Visitors leaving the motorway to enter La Laguna will notice a large statue near the intersection. This is a sculpture of Padre José de Anchieta, a gift from the Brazilian government. Anchieta was born in La Laguna in 1534 and studied in Portugal. He then became a Jesuit missionary. He spent much of his life in Brazil where he took a special interest in the way of life of the indigenous tribes. Anchieta is believed to have converted more than two million South American natives to Christianity. He also founded the Brazilian city of São Paolo, now one of the largest in the world. Padre Anchieta died in Brazil in 1597.

Historical La Laguna

The best starting point for a walk around the historical area is in the **Plaza del Adelantado**. This shady square, with its central marble fountain, is surrounded by venerable buildings of interest. On the eastern side are the market, the law courts and the **Ermita San Miguel**, a monastery that dates back to the early 16th century. On the south side of the square is the **Birthplace of Father Anchieta**, the missionary who founded the city of São Paulo in Brazil, and the neoclassical **Ayuntamiento** (Town Hall), which was built in 1822. Another striking building is the **Palacio de Nava** which dates from 1590 and has a façade which shows a variety of architectural styles, including Baroque and neoclassical. The whole of one side of the plaza is taken up with the **Convent of Santa Catalina de Sienna**. It is set up in the 17th century and still has a community of cloistered nuns. Note the superb *ajimeces*, or enclosed wooden balconies. The convent's church has an impressive panelled *Mudéjar* ceiling and an unusual wood and silver altarpiece. The convent is open on 15 February each year for people to see the incorruptible body of María de Jesús, to whom miracles have been attributed.

Museo de Historia y Antropologia de Tenerife ★★★
Leave the Plaza del Adelantado on the north side along Calle de Nava y Grimón and then turn left into Calle San Agustín. Shortly on the right is the **Museo de Historia y Antropologia de Tenerife**, located in the Casa Lercaro, a fine 16th-century townhouse. Undoubtedly the best history museum in the Canary Islands, it traces the history of Tenerife from the Spanish Conquest to the present day and has a particularly good map collection (open Tuesday–Saturday, 09:00–20:00; Sunday–Monday, 10:00–17:00; admission charge). Next door to the museum is the **Palacio Episcopal**, an early 17th-century building which was a casino before it became a bishop's palace.

Iglesia de Nuestra Señora de la Concepción ★★★
At the end of Calle San Agustín, turn left and arrive at the Plaza de la Concepción, where you'll find La Laguna's oldest church and the oldest parish church on the island, the **Iglesia de Nuestra Señora de la Concepción**. It dates from the early years of the 16th century, but much of its early architecture has been swamped by the later Gothic, Renaissance and Baroque additions. The church's most distinctive feature is its Moorish-looking seven-tiered tower. Inside there is a fine *Mudéjar* ceiling,

> **LA LAGUNA'S UNIVERSITY**
>
> Until very recently, the university at La Laguna was the only such institution in the Canary Islands. It was founded in the early 18th century by the Augustinians and the original building was in Calle San Agustín in the old part of the city. A new campus was built in the 1950s on the south side of La Laguna. There are nearly 13,000 students, who certainly add to the vibrant atmosphere in the city. A second university has now been set up in Gran Canaria to cope with the demand in the archipelago.

▼ *Below: Lofty church spires reflect La Laguna's importance as a religious centre.*

NORTHEAST TENERIFE

THE CASA DEL VINO

A popular tourist attraction in northeast Tenerife is the Casa del Vino *La Baranda*. It is located in a 17th-century house between El Sauzal and Tacoronte and owned by the island government, tel: 922 57 25 35, www.tenerife.es/casa-vino There is a small museum and a video presentation describing the history of wine making in Tenerife. Visitors can sample a selection of the wines of the area and buy bottles of their choice. The Casa del Vino also has an excellent restaurant, where diners can eat on a terrace with splendid views along the coastline.

an 18th-century cedarwood pulpit and some beautifully carved choir stalls. There are also sculptures by Pérez and Estévez and some ornate *retablos*. One of the statues, that of San Juan Evangelista, is said to have begun to sweat on 6 May 1648, and continued to do so for 40 days. Nobody has produced a scientific explanation for this 'miracle'. In the baptistery at the side of the church is a font, made of Seville ceramics; there are claims that it was used to baptize the Guanche leaders. The church is usually open Monday–Friday, 10:00–12:00 and during services.

Cathedral ★★★

A return to the Plaza del Adelantado via Calle del Obispo Rey Redondo passes the **Cathedral**, located in a small square graced by lofty palms. Tenerife's only cathedral dates back to 1515, and for many years it was the parish church of Los Remedios. When the bishopric was created in 1818, the church was upgraded to a cathedral and a considerable amount of work was carried out, including the construction of a classical façade. The interior is rather gloomy, but it is worth seeking out the statues by Luján Pérez and also the grave of Alonso Fernández de Lujo, which can be found behind the high altar.

▶ ▶ *Opposite: The simple little church of San Pedro at El Sauzal, with its photogenic white dome.*
▶ *Right: A huge satellite dish at the hi-tech Museo de la Ciencia y el Cosmos.*

Iglesia de San Francisco ★★★

Another excursion north from the Plaza del Adelantado leads via Calle de Nava y Grimón to the impressive Plaza de San Francisco, where the main attraction is the **Iglesia de San Francisco**. In the sanctuary is the statue of Christ, the *Santísimo Cristo de la Laguna*, which is believed to have been brought to Tenerife by

Alonso Fernández de Lugo in 1520. The figure was carved in black oak from Flanders by a Sevillian sculptor. The statue, which is one of the most venerated in the Canary Islands, is brought out at Easter to lead the Holy Week processions.

The University Area ★★★

The modern part of La Laguna lies to the south of the city centre and is based around the **University**. The 13,000 or so students create a lively atmosphere in the city. Associated with the university is the **Canarian Astrophysics Institute**, which also runs observatories on Mount Teide and on the island of La Palma. Also owned by the university is the fascinating **Museo de la Ciencia y el Cosmos** (Museum of Science and the Cosmos), which is noted for its hands-on, hi-tech presentation. Amongst other things you can undertake a lie detector test, experience the sound heard by a foetus in its mother's womb, communicate with outer space, pass through a maze of mirrors and even see your own skeleton!

THE WEST OF THE REGION

There are a number of small towns in the west of the region that are worth a visit, including Tacoronte, El Sauzal, Tegueste and Tejina, to name just a few. Here the Anaga Mountains slope gently westward and the volcanic soil and the moist conditions provide excellent conditions for agriculture.

THE TROGLODYTE TENDENCY

That some of the inhabitants of Tenerife still live in caves would surprise many visitors. This fact is true, but not as simple as it first seems. In the village of **Chinamada** in a remote part of the Anaga Mountains, there are some 30 families living in 'cave houses'. From the outside they look like normal houses, but closer inspection shows that behind the windows and doors, the rest of the house extends back into the rocky hillside. There may, in fact, be several cave rooms and small chimneys may be detected above, taking away the smoke from fires and kitchens. Although no electricity has reached Chinamada, the use of batteries, bottled gas and even solar panels, means that the residents have all the mod cons required for 21st-century living. The caves also have their own natural form of air conditioning, with the temperatures remaining constant throughout the year.

NORTHEAST TENERIFE

SEEING IN THE NEW YEAR

It is the habit in Spain, including Tenerife, to celebrate the New Year rather more than Christmas. At the stroke of midnight on New Year's Eve it is the custom to drink champagne (or cava) and eat a grape for each strike of the clock. To consume 12 grapes and take a drink so quickly is not easy and usually leads to great hilarity. The 12 grapes are supposed to guarantee good times in the year ahead.

Tacoronte ★★★

Tacoronte is an important market town of around 17,000 inhabitants. It is believed to have gained its name from the Guanche word *tagoro*, which means 'meeting place'. Potatoes and other vegetables are produced around here, but the town is most famous for its wine. In this part of the country vines can be grown without irrigation and Tacoronte wines were the first in the Canary Islands to be granted a DOC (certificate of origin). Particularly well-known are their strong sherry-like Malvasia wines. Tacoronte also possesses two interesting churches, close to each other in the town centre. The **Iglesia de Santa Catalina** dates back to 1664 and has a distinctive black and white bell tower. The **Iglesia del Cristo de los Dolores** was once part of an Augustinian monastery. Look for its altar of Mexican silver and the superb coffered ceiling panels. The fiesta of Cristo de los Dolores in September celebrates the wine harvest.

El Sauzal ★★★

Another nearby town in the wine-producing area is **El Sauzal**, its name derived from the willow trees, or *sauces*, that grow in the vicinity. El Sauzal is located on the top of a steep 300m (984ft) cliff overlooking the Atlantic – head for the Mirador de la Garañona which gives superb views along the coastline. Another sight in El Sauzal which should not be missed is the **Iglesia de San Pedro**, notable for its Moorish-style white dome. A photograph of the church, with a snow-capped Mount Teide in the distance, can look stunning. A visit to the Botanical Gardens *Las Tosquillas* is also recommended. Set up in 1957, the gardens cover some 5000m^2 (5980 sq yd). There are 50 species of palms from all over the world and a unique collection of 80 different types of air carnations or Tillandsias. Free-flying parrots and cockatoos add to the ambience. Wine buffs will head for the **Casa del Vino** *La Baranda* located in a typical 17th-century farmhouse and the neighbouring **Casa de la Miel** (House of Honey), where the galleries offer interesting background information on how this local natural speciality is produced (both attractions are open daily except Mondays).

Just north of El Sauzal are the two coastal hamlets of **Mesa del Mar** and **El Pris**, which are reached by steep roads. Both have good fish restaurants.

Valle de Guerra ★★★

The road north of El Sauzal heads inland to the town of **Valle de Guerra**, which is surrounded by rich agricultural land producing bananas and cut flowers such as strelitzia. The main reason for coming here, however, is to visit the **Casa de Carta Ethnographic Museum**. It is located in a well-restored 17th-century mansion and is without doubt the best museum of its type in the Canary Islands. The house itself is superb, with courtyards, balconies and patios providing wonderful views of the surrounding countryside. The displays present Canarian rural life over the centuries, with examples of country crafts and historic equipment. Particularly impressive are the folk costumes from various parts of Tenerife and the other islands. The museum is open daily, 10:00–17:00.

▲ *Above: Banana production flourishes on Tenerife, particularly around the town of Valle de Guerra.*

Tegueste and Tejina ★★★

Just off the road to the north is the small town of **Tegueste**. This is another wine producing area and the gateway to some good walking country in the lower slopes of the Anaga Mountains. Tegueste's main claim to fame is that it has the best Canarian wrestling team on the island. It also has one of the most important romerias in Tenerife, when horse-drawn carts are decorated with fruit and vegetables. Nearby **Tejina**, on the eastern side of the Valle de Guerra, was once an important town for the production of sugar cane. This led to a local rum-making industry. The factory still operates, but the sugar cane is now imported from other countries.

▲ *Above: The promenade in the quiet resort of Bajamar in the north of Tenerife.*

LOW-KEY HOLIDAY RESORTS

The road now swings towards the coast arriving first at **Bajamar** (the name literally means 'down by the sea'). It has a marvellous position on a platform between the foothills of the Anaga Mountains and the sea cliffs. Bajamar was one of the earliest resorts to develop in Tenerife, but it suffers from a lack of a good beach and experiences strong winds and waves. As a result it cannot compete with the big resorts in the south and has remained fairly low key. However, many visitors, particularly mainland Spaniards and Germans, like the quiet atmosphere and return time and again. The same is true of the last resort along the coast road, **Punta del Hidalgo**, where there has been rather more high-rise development. The fierce winds mean that most swimming has to take place in hotel pools. There are good views of the Anaga Mountains, particularly the twin peaks of **Roque Dos Hermanos**. There is a well-marked footpath from Punta del Hidalgo leading up to the cave village of **Chinamada** – allow three hours for the ascent.

Best Times to Visit

The northeast of Tenerife can be visited throughout the year. The winter is cloudier than the summer, particularly in the Anaga Mountains, which faces the rain-bearing trade winds. Because of this it is important that you choose a clear day on which to visit the mountains, whatever time of year, as there are many wonderful views that will be missed under cloud cover.

Getting There

TITSA **buses** (www.titsa.com) run regularly from both Santa Cruz and Puerto de la Cruz to the main towns of the northeastern parts of Tenerife.

Getting Around

Although TITSA **buses** link the main towns of the northeast, the service can be patchy and infrequent. Many of the smaller villages have no bus connections at all. **Car hire** is clearly the best option for seeing the main sights of the area and getting to the more remote parts. In some areas there are still a few isolated villages that can only be reached on foot or by the use of off-road vehicles. Those without a car may have to resort to taxis, in view of the scarcity of buses.

Where to Stay

In many parts of the northeast of Tenerife, there is little choice of accommodation. The best possibilities are in

La Laguna and in the small holiday resorts on the northwest coast.

Mid-range

Nivaria, Plaza del Adelantado 11, La Laguna 38002, tel: 922 26 42 98, fax: 922 25 96 34, www.lagunanivaria.com This is a good location for those wishing to explore the old town of La Laguna.

Oceano Hotel Health Spa, Pacifico 1, Punta Hildalgo, tel: 922 15 60 00, fax: 922 15 63 52, www.oceano.de New hotel resort offering detox, thalassotherapy and day spa facilities.

Hotel Rural Costa Salada, Camino La Costa S/N, Finca Oasis, tel: 922 69 00 00, fax: 922 54 10 55, www.costasalada.com Small rural hotel overlooking the northern coast.

Budget

Aguere, Obispo Rey Redondo 55, La Laguna, tel: 922 31 40 36, fax: 922 63 16 33, www.hotelaguere.es This small hotel is situated in the heart of the old town of La Laguna.

Where to Eat

Although good restaurants are quite hard to find in the more remote rural areas, there is still plenty of choice in La Laguna and the northwest resorts.

Mid-range

Casa del Vino, restaurant of the Wine Museum, La Baranda, El Sauzal, tel: 922

56 38 86, www.casadelvinotenerife.com Terrace with sea view.

San Nicolas, Ctra. General Sauzal, El Sauzal, tel: 922 56 13 56, www.restaurantsannicolas.es Excellent fish restaurant.

La Hoya del Camello, Ctra. General del Norte 118, La Laguna, tel: 922 26 20 54. This is probably La Laguna's best restaurant.

Mirador Benijo, Caseria Benijo, tel: 922 59 02 17. Small fish restaurant atop the cliffs. Magnificent views from the terrace.

Budget

La Laguna has some excellent *tapas* bars, including:
Tasca Al-Andalus, Calle El Peso 1, tel: 822 02 35 45 and **El Rincon Del Guanche**, Avenida Lucas Vega, tel: 822 17 42 01.

Tours and Excursions

The two most popular excursions in the area are to the **Casa de Carta Ethnographic Museum** near Valle de Guerra and the **Casa del Vino la Baranda** near El Sauzal.

Useful Contacts

Tourist Information Centres, La Laguna: Calle la Carrera, tel: 922 63 11 94. There is a kiosk in the square, open 09:00–17:00 daily.
Tacoronte: Ctra. General Tacoronte-Tejina, tel: 922 57 00 15, open Mon–Fri 09:00–13:00.

4
The Northern Coast

The northern coastal area of Tenerife is undoubtedly the most attractive part of the island. The trade winds ensure that it is cloudier and wetter than the arid south of the island, but these conditions encourage prolific vegetation and the growth of sub-tropical crops such as bananas and oranges. In the centre of the region is Tenerife's second most important town of **Puerto de la Cruz**. It became the prime port on the north coast of the island after the destruction of Garachico by volcanic activity, but the heavy Atlantic swell and the lack of shelter meant that it soon lost business to Santa Cruz. Fortunately, Puerto then developed as Tenerife's first holiday resort. Despite the cloudy weather, particularly in winter, it attracts more tourists than any other resort. The island's most popular theme park, **Loro Parque**, is close by.

You can also visit the dignified old town of **La Orotava**, located on a broad, upland valley. It is noted for the colonial architecture of its houses and public buildings, with their flower-bedecked wooden balconies and shady courtyards. La Orotava is also famous for its 'flower carpets' at Corpus Christi. In the east of the area are the twin towns of **La Matanza de Acentejo** and **La Victoria de Acentejo**, the sites of battles between the troops of Alfonso Fernández de Lugo and the Guanche army in the 15th century.

To the west of Puerto Cruz is the well-known wine-producing area based around **Icod de los Vinos**, a town which is also famous for the venerable **Drago Milenario**, claimed to be the oldest on the island. Nearby is the coastal town of **Garachico**, once

ATLANTIC OCEAN
La Laguna
Puerto de la Cruz
SANTA CRUZ DE TENERIFE
La Orotava
Pico del Teide
3718 m
ATLANTIC OCEAN
Playa de las Américas
Los Cristianos

DON'T MISS

*** **Loro Parque:** most popular theme park.
** **Casa de los Balcones:** craft centre with traditional Canarian architecture in La Orotava.
** **Costa Martiánez:** Puerto's seafront complex of pools.
* **Drago Milenario** (Dragon tree) **at Icod:** over 1000 years old.
* **Jardín Botánico:** Puerto's Botanical Gardens.
* **The 'Flower Carpets' at La Orotava:** designs made of volcanic sand and flowers at the Corpus Christi festival.

◀ *Opposite: Costa Martiánez in Puerto de la Cruz was designed by César Manrique.*

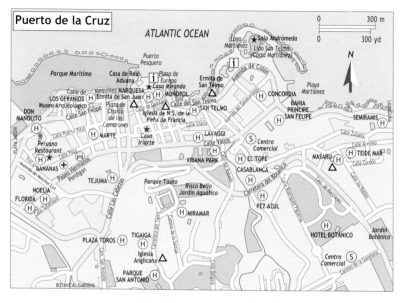

Puerto de la Cruz

ATLANTIC OCEAN

0   300 m
0   300 yd

N

Tenerife's largest port until volcanic lava engulfed the settlement in 1706. The remote peninsula to the west saw few tourists, but this is gradually changing as the attractions of villages such as **Buenavista del Norte** become more obvious.

The north coast provides some easy routes to Tenerife's main attraction, the volcanic mountain of **Mount Teide**, whose snow-capped peak looms over the region, providing endless photographic opportunities.

PUERTO DE LA CRUZ

Located at the northern end of the Orotava Valley, Puerto de la Cruz (or Puerto as it is more simply known) was founded in the early 17th century, when Philip IV selected it to be the main port of the district. It briefly increased in importance when a volcanic eruption and subsequent lava flow closed the rival port of Garachico to the west. However, the rocky coastline, Atlantic swell and the lack of a sheltered harbour, meant that its development would always be limited and it soon lost its influence to Santa Cruz in the east of the island.

CLIMATE

The north coast of Tenerife is on the windward side of the island and therefore receives more cloud and rain than the leeward south. **Rainfall** totals are nevertheless low and most precipitation comes in the winter months from November to February. Persistent **cloud** can, however, be a problem during this season. Most **sunshine** can be expected in the summer months from April to September.

By the late 19th century, Puerto de la Cruz was developing as a tourist centre as wealthy Victorian visitors from England stopped off on the voyage back from overseas. The British built the first hotels, such as the stately Monopol in the Plaza de Iglesia. The main development was to come in the 1960s, when charter flights began to bring tourists in large numbers. The more unsightly hotels and apartment blocks along the sea front at Puerto date from this time. The growth of resorts such as Los Cristianos and Playa de las Américas in the south of the island in the 1980s and 1990s provided new attractions for younger visitors.

Sights and Attractions ★★★

The hub of all the activity in Puerto de la Cruz is the **Plaza de Charco de los Camarones** (the Square of the Shrimp Pool), which was named after a tidal lagoon where the locals used to dredge for shrimps. Now raised and dry, the Plaza is shaded by massive Indian laurels and palm trees, the home of noisy feral parakeets. It is the haunt of shoe-shine boys, lottery ticket sellers and those with enough time for a game of outdoor chess. In the streets around the square are numerous Indian bazaars selling a range of bargain goods. The Plaza del Charco is also the site of the town's main taxi rank. Just off the Plaza is the **Museo Arqueológico** located in a 19th-century mansion. This small museum has a modest collection of remains from Guanche times, including a few mummies. Open Tuesday–Saturday, 10:00–13:00 and 17:00–21:00; Sunday, 10:00–13:00.

Leave the Plaza de Charco eastwards via the Calle de Quintana. On the left is the tiny **Ermita de San Juan**, which dates from the early years of the 17th century. The Calle de Quintana links up with Puerto's other attractive square, the more peaceful **Plaza de la Iglesia**. Dominating the square is the **Iglesia de Nuestra Señora de la Peña de Francia** (Church of Our Lady of the Rock of France).

▼ *Below: The beautiful coastline at Puerto de la Cruz brings visitors back year after year.*

The church was built between 1684 and 1697, with the tower added in 1898. The somewhat gloomy interior has a number of items of interest, including a *Mudéjar* ceiling, paintings by Luis de la Cruz, carvings by José Luján Pérez and an organ brought from London in 1814. Note, too, in a side chapel, the statue of the Virgen del Carmen, which is carried at the head of the fishermen's procession each July. Outside the church in the shady plaza is a delightful swan fountain and a statue of Agustín de Béthancourt, the engineer who was a native of Puerto de la Cruz. On the north side of the square are the town's oldest hotels, the **Hotel Marquesa**, which dates from 1712 and the **Hotel Monopol**, which was built in 1742. Both have attractive wooden balconies and courtyards. Just off the plaza, in Calle Iriarte is **Casa Iriarte**, the birthplace of the writer Tomás de Iriarte. This 18th-century house has some carved balconies and an attractive patio, but unfortunately the rather hotchpotch 'naval' museum on the upper floor and the souvenir shop on the ground floor do nothing to enhance one of the town's finest houses.

Most of the other attractions of Puerto are situated along the seafront. In the west is the **Playa Jardín**, a man-made beach backed by superb tropical gardens complete with sculptures. Nearby is the **Castillo de San Felipe**, all that remains of a line of defensive fortifications that once protected the port. The castle is now used for exhibitions and concerts. Further to the east is the **Puerto Pesquero**, or fishermen's harbour, a small-scale affair with a few token boats hauled up on a tiny shingle beach. There are some ancient buildings in this area, including the **Casa de Real Aduana** (the Royal Customs House) dating from 1620 and built in the traditional black and white stone. It was a working customs house until 1833. Opposite is the vibrantly coloured **Casa Miranda**, once the 18th-century home of Francisco de Miranda, who was prominent in Venezuela's fight for independence.

▼ *Below: The Jardín Botánico was set up by Carlos III in 1788 as an acclimatization site for tropical plants.*

◀ *Left: The Costa Martiánez, also known as the Lido San Telmo, occupies a large stretch of the seafront.*

Past the modern Plaza de Europa, the promenade known as Calle del San Telmo leads to the **Ermita de San Telmo**. This small chapel was founded by sailors in 1626 and dedicated to St Elmo, patron saint of seafarers. It has few treasures, but its simplicity never fails to impress. Just past the chapel is the **Costa Martiánez** (also known as the Lido San Telmo). Designed by the Lanzarote architect, artist and environmentalist, César Manrique, in 1977, the lido is a complex of pools, islands of volcanic rock, lawns and shrubbery which offers the perfect sheltered location for bathing and sunbathing. Many families spend the day here. There is a small entrance fee.

On the Higher Land to the South ★★★

For a superb viewpoint over the town, go to the **Mount Taoro** area. This is the location of the Grand Hotel Taoro, which was built by the British in the 1880s and in its heyday attracted guests such as Winston Churchill and Agatha Christie. Today the building stands closed up, neglected and more than a little forlorn, though. Adjacent to the hotel is a mirador in the **Parque Taoro**, with its aquatic gardens which, like the hotel, have seen better days and are need of some tender loving care.

By far the most interesting garden is the **Jardín Botánico**. The official name of this 2.5ha (6-acre) walled garden is La Orotava Acclimatization Garden. It was set up in 1788 by King Carlos III of Spain as a sort of halfway house for tropical plants to acclimatize before being sent on to mainland Spain. Few plants, in fact, survived the Spanish winters, but the acclimatization garden remains one of the main attractions of Tenerife. There are over 4000 plants here, including a massive 200-year-old South American rubber tree, scores

▶ *Loro Parque, with its wide variety of attractions, has become Tenerife's most visited tourist location.*

of orchids and other exotics. Visitors will also enjoy the feral parrots that nest here and the ornamental pond which is the centrepiece of the gardens. Open daily, 09:00–18:00.

Theme Parks ★★★

Visitors to Puerto de la Cruz, and indeed the whole of Tenerife, have two excellent theme parks to enjoy. On the western edge of the town is **Loro Parque** (Parrot Park). It was opened in 1982 and now has the largest collection of parrots, macaws, parakeets and similar species in the world. The park seems to expand annually and in addition to the parrots there is a dolphinarium, an aquarium with a walk-through plastic tunnel allowing eye to eye contact with sharks and rays, flamingo pools, a bat colony, monkey house and a Thai village – all set in superbly landscaped grounds. An attraction for the millennium was 'planet penguin' – an environment created for penguins in what has been described as 'the world's largest refrigerator'. The latest attraction is a group of orcas, or killer whales, obtained from a successful breeding programme of The US Sea World group. Loro Parque has, not surprisingly, proved to be the most popular tourist attraction in the Canary Islands with over 1.5 million visitors a year. The park can be reached by a free road train from the centre of Puerto de la Cruz. Open daily, 08:30–16:00 (last exit 18:45); tel: 922 37 38 41, www.loroparque.com

Between Puerto de la Cruz and La Orotava is **Pueblo Chico**, a world in miniature that will prove fascinating for children. Open daily, 10:00–17:00; tel: 922 33 48 60, www.pueblochico.com

EAST OF PUERTO DE LA CRUZ

On the eastern edge of the Orotava valley is the busy little market town of **Santa Ursula**, in the middle of a wine and banana producing area. It is worth stopping to view its parish church which dates from 1587 and has some fine sculptures and metalwork. You will also be impressed by the imposing Town Hall, fronted by young Dragon trees. Just outside Santa Ursula is the **Mirador de Humboldt**, named after the German explorer who was hugely impressed with this view across the Orotava valley. Further east is the Barranco de Acentejo, with the twin towns of **La Matanza** and **La Victoria**, which gained their names from the final battles between the Guanches and the invading Spanish. La Matanza translates as the 'massacre'. It was here that, in 1494, the Guanches lured the troops of Alonso Fernández de Lugo into an ambush in the Acentejo gorge. The Spanish lost over 900 men, most of them Canarian mercenaries. De Lugo escaped by wearing the blue cape of a foot soldier. He did not give up easily, however, and the following year he was back with a stronger force for a battle just 3km (2 miles) away from La Matanza. This time the Guanches, weakened by disease and in-fighting, were soundly defeated. De Lugo built a church on the site and the town that grew up around it was known as La Victoria (the Victory). Both La Mantanza an d La Victoria are agricultural centres and the area still makes pottery in the Guanche style.

WATER RESOURCES

Water is a scarce commodity in Tenerife. Supplies come from rainfall and melting snow on the upper slopes of Mount Teide. Much of the precipitation soaks underground, from where it has to be recovered by making tunnels into the hillsides or digging wells. From these sources the water runs through pipes, which can be seen everywhere festooned across the hillsides to individual farmhouses, which all have their storage tanks. It is a curious fact that all the water supply in Tenerife is in private hands and the release of water is strictly controlled and metered. Demand for water is great, particularly with the growth of the tourist industry, but so far, unlike the eastern islands of the Canaries, Tenerife has avoided reliance on desalination plants.

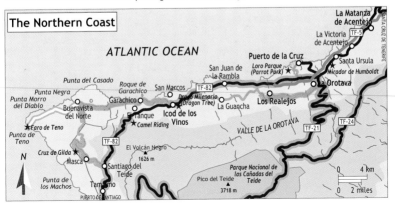

THE NORTHERN COAST

CRAFT CENTRE OF TENERIFE

La Orotava can justifiably be called the 'craft centre of Tenerife'. At Casa de los Balcones in Calle San Francisco is an embroidery and lace-making school with around 20 students a year. There is a museum upstairs, and craftsmen demonstrate basket and pottery making. The town has several art galleries and crafts boutiques in the streets of the town centre.

LA OROTAVA

The coat of arms of La Orotava has the words *villa muy noble y leal* – a most loyal and noble town. Few visitors to its old town would disagree. La Orotava was founded in the 16th century in the prosperous agricultural land of the Orotava Valley. It immediately attracted aristocratic immigrants (their coats of arms can be seen on many of the houses in the older part of the town) and a number of religious orders. The town has some superb examples of Spanish colonial architecture, with richly carved balconies and shady, flower-filled interior courtyards. Add to this some fine churches and convents, plus a few interesting museums and it can be seen why La Orotava makes such an interesting contrast with the coastal resorts.

The **Plaza de la Constitución**, the main square, has sweeping views towards the coast. At the side of the square is the monastery church of **San Agustín**. Dating back to 1694, it is now a music school. Above the plaza is the **Liceo de Taoro**. Built in the 19th century, it was once a school but is now a cultural centre offering a range of arts classes and is often open to the public for performances and exhibitions (www.liceodetaoro.es).

The late 19th-century **Ayuntamiento** (Town Hall) is situated southwest of the main square. The square in front of it and the surrounding streets mark the site of the 'flower carpets', an essential part of the Corpus Christi processions. Behind the Ayuntamiento is the **Hijuela del Botánico**, a beautiful garden which is an offshoot

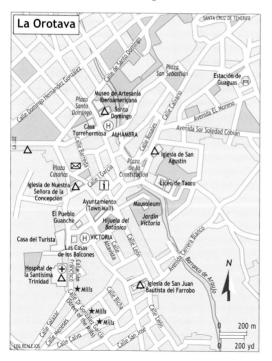

La Orotava

of the more famous botanical gardens in Puerto de la Cruz. It has a collection of over 3000 subtropical plants, including an impressive Dragon tree. Open Monday–Friday, 09:00–14:00.

A short stroll from the town hall is the **Iglesia de Nuestra Señora de la Concepción**, the town's most important church. Distinguished by its twin towers and dome, it was built in the late 18th century in Baroque style on the site of an earlier church destroyed by an earthquake. Inside there are statues by José Luján Pérez and Fernando Estévez (a native of La Orotava). Look for the marble altar and tabernacle (both of Italian origin and survivors from the original church) and the superbly carved choir stalls.

▲ *Above: Casa de los Balcones, a craft centre with a famous embroidery school.*

Head next to Calle San Francisco, a street that captures the atmosphere of Spanish colonial times. A favourite stop here is **Casa de los Balcones** (House of the Balconies). This building is in fact two 17th-century houses which were originally the home of a wealthy local family. They have since been joined together and today house an embroidery school. The exterior has a series of balconies with wrought iron railings. Inside is a charming courtyard with carved wooden balconies festooned with geraniums and ferns. The upper floor is a small museum. The ground floor has a workshop where visitors can watch craftspeople demonstrating pottery, basket making, embroidery and even cigar rolling. Many items are for sale and although prices are high, you can be sure that these are the genuine articles. Casa de los Balcones is open Monday–Friday, 08:30–18:30; Saturday 08:30–17:00; www.casa-balcones.com Small entrance charge.

Opposite is the **Casa del Turista** which dates from 1590 and was once part of a convent. Today it is a craft and gift shop along similar lines to Las Casas de los Balcones, with which it competes. The Casa del Turista has a convenient car park at the rear and its terrace has superb views over the Orotava Valley. Open Monday–Friday, 08:30–18:30; Saturday, 08:30–17:00; Sunday, 08:30–11:00.

FLOWER CARPETS

Try to be in La Orotava for the **Corpus Christi festival** (usually in late May). Scattering flowers on the pavements is not unusual in Spain to celebrate this special festival on the religious calendar, but it has become a fine art in La Orotava. Both flowers and volcanic soil are used for the decorations. The designs are geometric, floral, or depict scenes from the bible. No artificial colouring is used on either the flowers or the soil. The best displays centre on the Town Hall Square and the nearby streets. The first flower carpets in La Oratava date from the 1840s, but the tradition more or less died out until it was revived in 1906 for a visit by King Alfonso XIII.

THE NORTHERN COAST

▲ *Above: Iglesia de San Marcos at Icod, one of the most interesting churches on the island.*

At the upper end of Calle San Francisco is the **Hospital de la Santísima Trinidad** (Hospital of the Holy Trinity). It was once a Franciscan monastery before becoming a hospital in 1184. It now cares for the mentally handicapped. Its cloisters are occasionally open to the public – check with the tourist office. Just past the hospital, fork left into Calle Dr González García, popularly known as the **Street of the Mills**. There were once eleven working water mills here grinding cereals for making *gofio*. Only three survive today and they are now powered by electricity.

If time permits visit the **Museo de Artesanía Ibero-americana** in Plaza Santo Domingo. Located in a former monastery which was later used as a barracks, a prison and a school, it displays articles from countries across Latin America, including ceramics, musical instruments and textiles. The basement has a collection of Canarian costumes. The aim of the museum foundation is to promote arts and crafts both past and present so the galleries also offer an interesting collection by living artists and artisans from the Canaries and Latin America. Open Monday–Friday, 10:00–15:00.

WEST FROM PUERTO DE LA CRUZ

The first town on the road west from Puerto is **Los Realejos**, which has a population of around 30,000. The name means 'royal camp' and the town is divided into two sections, Realejo Alto (Upper Realejo) and Realejo Baja (Lower Realejo). Alto is the oldest of the two settlements and its church, which was built in 1498, is the most ancient in Tenerife. It is here that the defeated Guanche menceyes were forcibly baptized. Further west are the attractive agricultural towns of **San Juan de Rambla** and **La Guancha**, which have little to detain the tourist in a hurry.

ICOD DE LOS VINOS

After 10km (6 miles) the town of **Icod de los Vinos** is reached. As its name suggests, it is in the centre of a wine producing area and its white wine has its own denomination of origin. The wine festival at the end of November can be a riotous affair. The wineries have an open day and it is a custom for youths to hurtle down the steep Calle Calvario on wooden sledge boards. Most people come to Icod to see **Drago Milenario** the 1000-year-old Dragon tree, which is over 16m (52ft) high. It is claimed that the Guanche menceyes administered justice from beneath its branches. To preserve it, the authorities have re-routed a road and supported the trunk with concrete and steel bars.

There is much more to see in Icod. Near the Dragon tree is a shady square with laurels, jacarandas and palms surrounding the 16th-century Church of **San Marcos**. The exterior shows elements of Gothic, Renaissance and Baroque architecture. Do look inside this five-naved church with its *artesonado* ceiling, some fine *retablos* and a huge silver cross from Mexico which is 2m (6ft) high and weighs 47kg (103lb). It is reckoned to be the largest silver filigree cross in the world. A steep lane leads from the church up to the Plaza de la Constitución. It is well worth the climb as the square looks much as it would have done 200 years ago. It is full of fine old trees and surrounded by ancient buildings and bodegas. Another attraction, just a few yards from the Dragon tree, is the **Mariposario del Drago** (also known as The Butterfly Zoo), a fascinating butterfly park. Here are hundreds of exotic species from all over the world and it is possible to see all the stages of the life cycle, from egg to butterfly. Open daily, in winter 10:00–18:00; in summer 10:00–19:00; tel: 922 81 51 67, www.mariposario.com

In the Plaza de la Constitución, near the Dragon tree, is the Artlandya Museum. Located in an old Canarian mansion with a charming patio, it displays a range of dolls, puppets and teddy bears (www.artlandya.com). Open Tuesday–Sunday, 10:00–18:00. Entrance fee.

▼ Below: Drago Milenario (the Dragon tree) at Icod, reputed to be the oldest in Tenerife.

THE NORTHERN COAST

▶ *Opposite: Camel safaris are a popular tourist attraction on Tenerife.*
▼ *Below: The Castillo de San Miguel at Garachico, which survived the lava in 1706.*

GARACHICO

The road westward from Icod gives some superb views down over the coastal town of Garachico, with its distinctive rocky offshore islet, known as the Roque de Garachico. The town was founded by Genoese merchants in 1496 and for many years was the main commercial port of the north coast, exporting wine and sugar to the New World. Disaster struck in 1706 when the nearby Volcán Negro erupted and large parts of Garachico were engulfed in lava, which completely blocked up the port. The town has a long history of misfortune as it has also been afflicted with earthquakes and an outbreak of the plague. However, the town's motto is 'glorious in adversity' and it has continued to thrive, although never regaining its former dominence.

It is well worth strolling around Garachico to take in the sights. An obvious landmark is the **Castillo de San Miguel**, a sturdy fortress which somehow survived the advancing lava. It was built in 1575 to defend the port against pirates but today stands amidst the petrified lava flows. Head next for the **Plaza Glorieta de San Francisco**, the town's main square. There are a number of notable buildings here. The former **Convent of San Francisco** now functions as the Casa de Cultura and hosts a variety of exhibitions and other events. The old convent also houses the **Museo de las Ciencias Naturales**, which has a fascinating account of the 1706 eruption. Take a look at the convent's church, the **Iglesia de San Francisco**, which has a distinguished *Mudéjar* ceiling. Also in the Plaza is the restored **Palacio de los Condes de la Gomera**, the one-time home of the Counts who also owned the castle. Another square nearby is the **Plaza de Arriba**, where we find Garachico's most important church, the Renaissance-style **Iglesia de Santa Ana**. The original building was mostly destroyed in the volcanic eruption and the

72

present church was rebuilt between 1714 and 1721. It has some fine *retablos* (which is not surprising as Garachico is a religious carving centre) plus some statues by Luján Pérez. Don't leave the Plaza de Arriba without finding the Statue of Simon Bolivar, who did much in the fight for South American independence from Spain. If you are wondering why Bolivar's statue

is in Garachico, it is because his mother was born in the town. Finally, take a stroll around the Parque Puerto de Tierra. In these attractive gardens is the huge 16th-century gateway that once marked the entry to the former port. For a good photo opportunity head to the west of the town to a mirador which has a monument to the Emigrants of the town.

The main road now heads southwest towards the pass which leads down to the arid southwest coast. The only settlement of note is **El Tanque**, which is well known for its Camel Centre (www.camellocenter.es). Visitors are dressed in Arab clothing and taken on a camel safari, pausing to take mint tea in what is claimed to be a genuine Bedouin tent.

The minor road from Garachico heads west towards the northwestern tip of the island. The land here is known as the **Teno Massif** and it was one of the earliest parts of Tenerife to be formed, probably some 7 million years ago. It is the most inaccessible and most sparsely populated part of the island. To the north of the road from Garachico is the **Montaña de Taco reservoir**, the largest on the island and, unusually, sited in the crater of a volcano. The only settlement of any size is **Buenavista del Norte**. It has a pleasant main square, but has little else of interest except the main church of **Nuestra Señora de los Remedios**, which has a 17th-century painting by Alonso Cano and some ornate *retablos*. The town's lighthouse, with its corkscrew-shaped tower is also of interest. Just 11km (7 miles) west of Buenavista is the volcanic headland of **Punta de Teno**, with its distinctive lighthouse and renowned sunsets.

THE WORLD OF THE BANANA

Tenerife's economy is full of examples of 'boom and bust'. The latest agricultural product to suffer is the banana. It was first used as a cash crop for export in the 1870s, but the trade suffered badly during the Spanish Civil War and later during World War II. While it is still the single most important crop in Tenerife it has strong competition from many Central American republics, where the plantations are run by large American corporations. The Canary Island banana is small and Europeans tend to prefer the larger Central American fruit. In Tenerife, the banana also requires irrigation and many people feel that the precious water would be better used in the more economically productive tourist industry. Some tourist information still mentions the **Bananera el Guanche** theme park near La Orotava – don't bother looking for it, as it closed in 2007.

THE NORTHERN COAST AT A GLANCE

BEST TIMES TO VISIT
The northern coast is a popular all-year-round destination, but visitors should bear in mind that this is the cloudiest and wettest side of the island, particularly in the wintermonths. The summer sees rather less cloud and rain and does not experience the high temperatures found in the south of the island. For this reason summer is generally considered to be the best time to visit the area.

GETTING THERE
The nearest airport is Los Rodeos (Tenerife Norte) just west of Santa Cruz, but most visitors arrive at Reina Sofía Airport (Tenerife Sur) in the east of the island. From here it is a one-hour drive by coach or car to Puerto de la Cruz, using the motorway system. Ferries from the other islands arrive at Santa Cruz and Los Cristianos, from where buses link with Puerto de la Cruz.

GETTING AROUND
The TITSA bus company runs services from Puerto de la Cruz to other places along the north coast. **Car hire** is cheap and there are many hire companies in Puerto de la Cruz. The motorway system enables drivers to reach all parts of the island quickly, but visitors should be prepared for narrow roads and hairpin bends in the more remote areas.

WHERE TO STAY
Luxury
Hotel Botánico, Calle Richard J. Yeoward, Puerto de la Cruz, tel: 922 38 14 00, www.hotel botanico.com Situated on the hill above the town close to the botanical gardens. Pool.
Bahia Principe San Felipe, Avda de Colón 22, Puerto de la Cruz, tel: 922 38 33 11, www.bahia-principe.com Modernised, with a wide range of facilities and services.
Tigaiga, Parque Taoro 28, Puerto de la Cruz, tel: 922 38 35 00, fax: 922 38 4055, www.tigaiga.com Luxury hotel on a hilltop overlooking Mount Teide and the ocean.
Best Semiramis, Calle Leopoldo Cólogan Zuleata, Puerto de la Cruz, tel: 922 37 32 00, fax: 922 37 31 93, www.besthotels.es A conveniently placed hotel with good views of the coast. Pool.

Mid-range
Monopol, Calle Quintana 15, Puerto de la Cruz, tel: 922 38 46 11, fax: 922 37 03 10, www.monopol.vikahotel.com Historic hotel in the Plaza de la Iglesia.
Marquesa, Calle Quintana 11, Puerto de la Cruz, tel: 92238 31 51, fax: 922 38 69 50, www.hotelmarquesa.com
San Telmo, Calle San Telmo 18, Puerto de la Cruz, tel: 922 38 58 53, fax: 922 38 59 91. Family-run hotel located on the waterfront.
San Roque, Calle Estaban de Ponte 32, San Roque,

Garachico, tel: 922 13 34 35, www.hotelsanroque.com In the attractive old town.
Victoria, Calle Hermano Apolinar 8, La Orotava, tel: 922 33 16 83, fax: 922 32 05 19, www.hotelruralvictoria.com Small hotel in a converted and modernized manor house.

Budget
Los Geranios, Calle de Lomo 14, Puerto de la Cruz, tel: 922 38 28 10, www.pensionlos geranios.com Comfortable guesthouse in a quiet part of town.
Silene Pension, Calle Tomás Zerolo 9, La Orotava 38300, tel: 922 33 01 99, www.sile neorotava.es 19th-century guesthouse in the historic centre of La Orotava.

Rural
El Patio, near Garachico, tel: 922 13 32 80, www.hotel patio.com Rural plantation home that has been in the family since 1507.

WHERE TO EAT
Puerto de la Cruz has a huge variety of restaurants, from elegant international establishments to American fast-food joints and humble *tapas* bars. It is worth searching out Venezuelan restaurants, run by returning immigrants. Elsewhere in the region Canarian food is the norm.

Luxury
Marquesa, Calle Quintana, Puerto de la Cruz, tel: 922 38

31 51. Elegant dining on the hotel balcony overlooking the Plaza de la Iglesia.

La Parilla, Hotel Botánico, Avda Richard Yeoward, tel: 922 38 14 00. High-class hotel restaurant serving international food.

Magnolia, Avenida Marques Villanueve del Prado, Puerto de la Cruz, tel: 922 38 56 14, www.restaurantmagnolia. com Catalan style seafood.

Mil Sabores, Calle Cruz Verde, Puerto de la Cruz, tel: 922 37 22 47. Creative Mediterranean dishes. Patio dining and a pretty indoor space.

Mid-range

Isla Baja, Calle Esteban de Ponte, Garachico, tel: 922 83 00 08. Seafront fish restaurant.

Carmen, Plaza de la Iglesia, Icod de los Vinos, tel: 922 81 05 31. Canarian food, in a traditional town house.

Regulo, Calle Pérez Zamora 16, Puerto de la Cruz, tel: 922 38 45 06, www.rest auranteregulo.com Specialist seafood restaurant.

La Carta, Calle Felipe 53, Puerto de la Cruz, tel: 922 38 15 92. Small restaurant with creative cuisine, fish and some vegetarian options.

Bodegon Matias, Carretera Parque Nacional del Teide, Los Pinos, Los Orotava, tel: 922 32 02 59, www.bo degonmatias.eu Traditional Canarian dishes served with modern flair.

Budget

Café de Paris, San Telmo 10, Puerto de la Cruz, tel: 922 38 40 00. Seafront, French-style café serving excellent breakfasts with croissants.

Bodega Julian, Calle Mequinez 20, Puerto de la Cruz, tel: 686 55 63 15. Small family owned eatery serving excellent local dishes and *tapas*.

Tours and Excursions

Puerto de la Cruz is the main centre for the departure of excursions in the area. The main local theme park is **Loro Parque**, tel: 922 37 38 41, www.loroparque.com, with the world's largest collection of parrots and similar birds, plus dolphins, penguins and a host of other attractions. Many enjoy the **Botanical Gardens** on the southern outskirts of Puerto, or a camel safari at the **Camel Centre** at El Tanque (tel: 922 13 61 91, www. camellocenter.es). Further afield is the unmissable Mount Teide National Park, which can easily be reached by hire car or on a coach excursion.

Diving: Diving lessons are available at Dive Centre ATLANTIK Hotel Maritim,

tel: 922 36 28 01, www.scubacanarias.com

Mountain Biking: Excursions by mountain bike can be arranged. Bikes available for hire. Contact Mountainbike Active, Calle Puerto Viejo 44, Edf. Don Juan, Puerto de la Cruz, tel: 922 37 60 81, www.mtb-active.com

Shopping: The historic centre of La Orotava is a centre of arts and crafts, with small boutiques selling jewellery, clothing and ceramics, and mainsream art. Puerto de la Cruz has an excellent range of souvenir shops, plus boutiques selling summer and resortwear.

Useful Contacts

There are **Tourist Information Centres** in these towns:
Puerto de la Cruz, Casa de la Aduana, tel: 922 38 60 00.
La Orotava, Calle Calvario 4, tel: 922 32 30 41.
Garachico, Avda Republica de Venezuela, tel: 922 13 34 61.
Disabled Travellers:
Shop in Puerto de la Cruz for disabled travellers – hire out wheelchairs and provide a repair service. Contact Le Ro, Apartamentos Martina, Calle Ruiman 23, Puerto de la Cruz, tel: 922 37 33 01.

LA LAGUNA	J	F	M	A	M	J	J	A	S	O	N	D
AVERAGE TEMP. °F	53	53	55	57	59	62	66	68	66	64	59	55
AVERAGE TEMP. °C	12	12	13	14	15	17	19	20	19	18	15	13
RAINFALL in	3.6	2.9	2.6	1.6	0.8	0.4	0.2	0.2	0.6	2.4	4.5	4.1
RAINFALL mm	91	74	66	41	20	10	5	5	15	61	114	104

5
The Arid East

Visitors arriving at the **Reina Sofía Airport (Tenerife Sur)** on Tenerife's south coast can scarcely have a worse introduction to the island. The landscape is arid and brown, with the gentle slopes covered with cactus-like euphorbia plants, so that the scenery resembles the coast of nearby Africa. Soulless industrial estates surround the airport interspersed with wind farms to generate electricity. There are numerous patches of *plasticultura* – greenhouses made of plastic netting in which bananas are grown under irrigation. Fortunately, it is only necessary to go 10–15km (6–9 miles) inland to find that the scenery improves. Steep-sided *barrancos* lead to attractive market towns surrounded by cultivation terraces, roadside wild flowers and extensive forests.

The route southwest from Tenerife's other airport, **Los Rodeos (Tenerife Norte)**, presents a much more attractive picture, with a road leading along the spine of Tenerife, the **Cumbre Dorsal**, making this the most attractive route to the Mount Teide National Park.

There is little development along the east coast, despite the motorway that hugs the shore. An exception is the town of **Candelaria**, the basilica of which contains the image of St Candelaria, which attracts pilgrims from all over the Canary Islands and even further afield. Another small, but developing town is **El Médano**, the nearest resort to the airport and the haunt of windsurfers. In the extreme south of the area is the **Costa del Silencio**, with small fishing villages such as **Las Galletas** and some of the best golf courses in the archipelago.

ATLANTIC OCEAN
La Laguna
Puerto de la Cruz
SANTA CRUZ DE TENERIFE
La Orotava
Pico del Teide
3718 m
Playa de las Américas
ATLANTIC OCEAN
Los Cristianos

DON'T MISS

** **The Pyramids at Güímar:** ancient pyramids or just a heap of stones?
** **The Basilica and statues at Candelaria:** the Canary Islands prime pilgrimage site.
* **The Miradors along the Cumbre Dorsal:** giving views to either side of the island and up to Mount Teide.
* **Wind Surfing at El Médano:** one of the top ten sailboarding locations in the world.

◀ *Opposite: The Virgin in the Basilica at Candelaria attracts pilgrims from all over the world.*

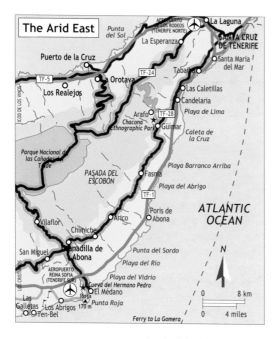

The Arid East

THE CUMBRE DORSAL

TF-24 leaves La Laguna and heads up onto the backbone of the island, Cumbre Dorsal, a ridge which runs in a southwesterly direction up to the Mount Teide National Park (described in Chapter 7). The ridge rises from 600m (2000ft) to reach a height of about 2000m (7500ft) and there are numerous miradors along it (*see* panel, this page), giving fine views to both the north and south of the island. The Cumbre Dorsal is in fact a chain of ancient volcanoes that have long since become extinct and also eroded. At the lower levels of the ridge there are a number of scattered hamlets that collectively go under the name of **El Rosario**. The largest settlement in the region is **La Esperanza**, which is well known for its restaurants specializing in country dishes of pork, veal and rabbit. These restaurants are very popular at weekends with the *Santacruceros*. On the higher land around La Esperanza is Tenerife's largest pine forest, which has a number of hiking trails and picnic spots.

THE EASTERN ROUTES

Drivers travelling along the eastern side of Tenerife have a choice of two routes. For those in a hurry there is the **TF1 Motorway**. For visitors with more time on their hands there is the higher, parallel **TF-28**, which is considerably slower and includes many dangerous bends. However, it does pass through some attractive scenery and numerous sleepy market towns.

CUMBRE DORSAL'S MIRADORS

Tenerife's most impressive *miradores*, or viewpoints, are those along the **Cumbre Dorsal**. Leaving La Laguna, the first stop should be at the **Montaña Grande** at 1120m (3675ft), with superb views of Santa Cruz and La Laguna. A little further is the **Mirador Pico de las Flores** at 1310m (4298ft) with even better views in the same direction. Some 7km (4 miles) further is the **Mirador Otuño**, which affords fine views of Mount Teide and north Tenerife. A short diversion from the main road leads to the **Mirador de las Cumbres**, with a vista of the southern half of Tenerife.

THE INLAND ROUTE

The first town of any importance on the route of the TF-28 is **Güímar**, the capital of an old Guanche district. The broad Güímar Valley extends seaward and its fertile soil has been terraced for the cultivation of bananas, tomatoes and potatoes. There are also considerable areas of vineyards and Güímar wines have their own DOC. Prominent in the valley is the unmistakable shape of Güímar volcano. The town of Güímar has around 18,000 inhabitants and acts as a market centre for the region. In the main square is the 18th-century church of San Pedro, which is well worth a look. Nearby is the former Convent of San Domingo, which is now the Town Hall. Look for the plaque on a house in the square that marks the birthplace of Isidro Quintero Acosta, who was active in South American politics and introduced the cultivation of cochineal to the Canary Islands. A tortuous road runs northwards from Güímar through the sleepy village of **Arafo** to link up with the Cumbre Dorsal route.

▼ *Below: Mirador de Don Martín, one of scores of viewpoints on the island.*

THE ARID EAST

Most people come to Güímar, however, to visit the **Pirámides de Güímar Ethnographic Park**, just north of the town. In the early 1990s, some stone pyramids were excavated here. They caught the attention of Thor Heyerdahl, a Norwegian anthropologist, who was convinced that they were of significance and had similarities with other pyramids in Mexico and Peru. He persuaded his friend, the shipping line owner Fred Olsen, to buy the site and they set up an ethnographical museum here. Recent excavations have turned up a cave that was inhabited by the Guanches and a number of their artefacts have been found, including a basalt sphere. Visitors should be aware, however, that the pyramids are controversial and many authorities consider that they are simply stones that were piled up by local farmers as they cleared their fields for terracing. Other theories link the terrace orientation with winter and summer solstices and even 19th-century freemasonry! Whatever the verdict, the site makes a very interesting visit. Apart from the excellent museum there are some reed boats, including the replica of Heyerdahl's reed boat *Ra II*. The museum is open daily, 09:30– 18:00; tel: 922 51 45 10, www.piramidesdeguimar.net

The next agricultural village is **Fasnia**, which has some interesting stone aqueducts in the vicinity. Fasnia was almost destroyed in 1705 when the local volcano erupted, but luckily the lava stopped just short of the village. Next along is the

◀ *Left: Statues of Guanche chiefs line the waterfront at Candelaria.*
◀◀ *Opposite: A stone pyramid at Güímar's Ethnographic Park.*

Arico area with the villages of Lomo de Arico, Arico el Viejo and Arico el Nuevo. The only feature to detain tourists here is the village church of San Juan Bautista at Lomo, which has some fine painted panels and an unusual bell tower. A further 15km (9 miles) will bring you to **Granadilla de Abona**, another agricultural centre that markets local tomatoes, potatoes and peppers for tourist centres of the coast. Granadilla has an 18th-century church and a ruined convent that was founded in the 17th century. From Granadilla, the TF-21 runs northwards in a series of hairpin bends to **Vilaflor** and the Mount Teide National Park. The attractive village of Vilaflor lies at a height of 1400m (4593ft), making it the highest settlement in Tenerife. Its clear air helps people with respiratory problems and the village has become something of a health resort. Vilaflor is well known for its lace making and for the spring water which is bottled nearby and distributed all over the island. Vilaflor is also the starting point for hikes to the so-called **Paisaje Lunar** (Lunar Landscape), which is an area of soft white rock that has been eroded into strange shapes. The flanks of the rock walls have been worn smooth with many topped by diminutive rock 'chimneys', making an impressive sight. The final settlement along the inland road is **San Miguel**, which gets its name from the Archangel Michael, the patron saint of the town, whose statue is in the 18th-century church. The town is an important farming centre and traditional pottery has also seen a revival here.

WHAT'S IN A NAME?

Vilaflor could be translated as 'village flower', but the town did not always have this romantic name. It was known to the Guanches as *Chasna*. The present name dates back to the Conquest. A conquistador, Captain Pedro de Bracamonte, fell in love with a beautiful young Guanche girl. On his deathbed, he is said to have uttered the words *'Vi la flor de Chasna'* (I have seen the flower of Chasna). The words are now on the town's coat of arms.

HERMANO PEDRO

Brother Pedro was a monk who hailed from the village of Vilaflor, where he was born in 1619. He was forced out of his birthplace and went to live a hermit-like existence in a cave near El Médano (close to the present airport runway). Hermano Pedro eventually emigrated to Central America where he formed the Bethlehemite order of monks. Their missionary work was influential throughout Latin America. Hermano Pedro was canonized in 1980 and his cave has become a place of pilgrimage, with mass being celebrated there twice a year.

THE ARID EAST

THE COASTAL ROUTE

The TF1 Motorway follows a route closer to the sea through the arid coastal plain. The first town of importance is **Candelaria**, a municipality of approximately 25,000 people. It is well known as the main centre of pilgrimage in the archipelago. The object of all this adoration is the **Statue of the Virgin of Candelaria**. The original statue was found on the beach in Guanche times before being acquired by the Spanish *conquistadores*. The image was originally kept in a cave, until a sanctuary, the **Basilica de Nuestra Señora de Candelaria**, was built in 1526. This was replaced in the 19th century by the present church and adjacent convent.

The statue, however, is not the original one, as this was washed out to sea by a tidal wave in 1826. The present image is in fact a copy of a copy that was sculpted by Fernanado Estévez. This does not seem to worry the pilgrims who come from far and wide for the celebrations on 15 August to pay homage to the Black Madonna (*see panel, page 84*). There is a large plaza in front of the church, providing an ideal venue for the event. On the seaward side of the plaza is a row of nine imposing bronze statues mounted on plinths of volcanic lava. These represent the Guanche leaders, or *menceyes*, at the time of the Spanish Conquest. The original statues were made of sandstone and were quite badly eroded. If you would like to see these, they can be found on the newly built *rambla* to the north of the town. This route makes a lovely stroll with plenty of cafés offering excellent cakes and coffee.

The town of Candelaria itself is pleasant enough, with a very interesting old town and some attractive low-rise apart-ment blocks on the northern side. Unfortunately, the beach consists of coarse black volcanic sand and there are some dangerous currents, so it cannot really be recommended for swimming, despite a tidal pool.

Tourist developments along this stretch of the coast are few and far between, but one place that looks likely to expand is **Poris de Abona**. At present it is just a small fish-ing village, but already a holiday resort has been built on the outskirts.

Further south and close to the airport is **El Médano**, which is rapidly becoming a tourist centre. It has one of the best beaches on the island, but its main drawback is wind. The trade winds are persistently strong here and the beach sand even penetrates hotel bedrooms. This does not bother the

COSTA DEL GOLF?

Tenerife has been slow to realize the potential of the game of golf to attract tourists. Indeed, until the late 1980s there was only one golf club on the island – the **Royal Golf Club of Tenerife**, 16km (10 miles) from Santa Cruz in the north of the island. This was set up by the British in 1932 and is the second oldest golf club in Spain. In 1987 **Golf de Sur** was opened on the Costa del Silencio, followed two years later by the nearby **Amarilla Golf**. In 1994 the nine-hole **Los Palos** came into operation. There are other courses at **Buenavista del Norte**, **Guia de Isora**, **Costa Adeje**, **Puerto de la Cruz** and **Las Americas**, so that visiting golfers now have a choice of ten courses, while **Tecina Golf** on La Gomera is only a 40-minute ferry ride away. For further information try www.golf-in-tenerife.com

◀◀ *Opposite: The Basilica de Nuestra Señora de Candelaria which dates from the 19th century.*
◀ *Left: Farms growing crops under plastic are a common feature of the southeastern parts of Tenerife.*

THE ARID EAST

▶ Right: Palm trees swaying in
the wind at the Buenavista del
Norte golf course.

windsurfers who swarm to this site – they rate it as one of
the top ten in the world for this sport. There are windsurfing
schools and plenty of shacks where equipment can be hired.
El Médano's beaches are divided by the **Montaña Roja**, a striking red-coloured remnant of a volcano, some 170m (550ft)
high. The village of El Médano has some quaint, narrow streets
with a central square, around which are a number of bars and
restaurants. Adjacent to the square is a small sheltered beach
that is popular with families. It is worth walking to the west of
the village to see the **Cueva del Hermano Pedro**, the cave of
the hermit and missionary Brother Pedro. The proximity of the
airport and its noisy jets, plus the persistent wind, mean that
it is unlikely that El Médano will ever become a major resort
like its neighbours to the west.

BEST TIMES TO VISIT
This is the driest part of the island and sunshine is guaranteed throughout the year, but be prepared for some persistent wind. The inland areas tend to have a layer of cloud that can be slow to clear in the winter. The east coast is an all-year-round destination.

GETTING THERE
The east coast has the benefit of being the part of the island that is closest to the international airport, so incoming visitors do not have far to travel. Tourists based in the Puerto de la Cruz area can reach the east coast by service bus or car in under an hour.

GETTING AROUND
The TITSA bus company (www.titsa.com) runs regular services along the coast road linking the airport with Santa Cruz and the resorts to the west, but the services to the inland towns are less frequent. Car hire is the best way of covering the area.

WHERE TO STAY
Accommodation is thin on the ground along the east coast, particularly inland. Rooms at resorts such as Ten Bel tend to be pre-booked by tour parties. The best bets are at El Médano and Candelaria.

El Médano
Playa Sur Tenerife, Playa del Médano, tel: 922 17 61 20, www.hotelplayasurtenerife.com Popular with windsurfers.

El Médano, Playa del Médano, tel: 922 17 70 00, fax: 922 17 60 48, www.medano.es At the other end of the town on a small headland. Another windsurfers' favourite.
KN Hotel Arenas Del Mar, Avenue Europa 2, El Médano, tel: 922 17 98 30, fax: 922 17 76 11, www.knhoteles.com Contemporary minimalist interiors in this new property.

Candelaria
Because of the August pilgrimage, there is a range of accommodation here.
Catalonia Punta del Rey, Avenida Generalisimo 165, Las Calletillas, Candelaria, tel: 922 50 18 99, www.hotelescatalonia.com Large modern hotel with pool and sea views.
Camping Nauta, Cañada Blanca, Las Galletas, tel: 922 78 51 18. Tenerife's only official fully equipped camp site.

Inland
Hotel Rural Finca Salamanca, Carre. Güímar, Pertito 2, Güímar, tel: 922 51 45 30, fax: 922 51 40 61, www.hotelfincasalamanca.com Twenty room property surrounded by farmland.

WHERE TO EAT
The inland towns have few possibilities for eating out, but the coastal resorts offer a good choice.

El Médano
Gastrobar la Plaza, Avenida Jose Miguel Galvan Bello 6,

Plaza Roja, tel: 645 54 93 67. Great selection of *tapas*, pasta and salads.

Candelaria
El Autentico, Calle Santo Domingo 21, Las Cuevecitas, tel: 649 15 28 11. Authentic Canarian cuisine at a finca in the hills above the town.

Los Abrigos
Los Roques, Calle la Marina 16, 38618 Los Abrigos, tel: 922 74 94 01, www.restaurantelroques.com Fresh fusion food with harbourside views.
La Langostera, Calle la Marina 18, Los Abrigos, tel: 922 17 03 02. Best of a number of harbourside seafood restaurants.

TOURS AND EXCURSIONS
Those staying on the Costa del Silencio will find that there are many organized tours to the **Teide National Park** and the various theme parks to the north of Los Cristianos. Visitors wishing to see the so-called pyramids at Güímar will need to hire a car. Close to the airport is the **Karting Club Tenerife**, claiming to be Europe's number one go-kart circuit; tel: 922 73 07 03, www.kartingtenerife.com

USEFUL CONTACTS
Tourist information Centres, Candelaria:
Avenida Constitucion 7, tel: 922 03 22 30
Güímar: Avenida Obispo Pérez Cácares 18, tel: 922 51 15 90.

6
The Southwest

Before the 1960s this part of Tenerife was largely deserted, but then its potential for tourism was realized and development has continued unabated ever since. Although the coastal area has few scenic attractions the region's main advantage is its weather. It can be cloudy and indeed occasionally wet inland, but the coastal strip benefits from almost unbroken sunshine throughout the year – an advantage not enjoyed by resorts on the northern coast.

The three main resorts in the southwestern part of the island are **Los Cristianos**, **Playa de las Américas** and **Costa Adeje**. The former is based around an old fishing port, but Playa de las Américas and Costa Adeje were built almost entirely from scratch. The three resorts have now joined up to form a huge tourist conurbation, which is probably the largest on Spanish territory. Apartment blocks and hotels sprawl up the hillsides and sand has been imported to improve the beaches. Clubs, discos and bars abound providing everything for the younger tourist looking for a lively time. A number of **theme parks** have appeared in the surrounding area, which are very popular with families and easily reached on the free shuttle buses. There is also a full range of **water sports** available for the more active visitor.

Development is now moving northwards along the coast, towards the quieter and more up-market resorts of **Puerto de Santiago** and **Los Gigantes**, set against the impressive volcanic cliffs. Further inland, the landscape is arid and uninspiring. An exception is the **Barranco del Infierno**, a deep

Don't Miss

** Barranco del Infierno: enjoy some easy hiking along a stupendous gorge.
** Las Aguilas del Teide: best of the theme parks.
** Los Gigantes: the towering cliffs of volcanic basalt to the north of Puerto de Santiago.
** Masca: remote and picturesque village among great walking country in the Teno Mountains.
* Siam Park: pools, chutes and slides in this waterpark on the outskirts of Playa de las Américas.

◀ *Opposite: The village of Masca among stunning scenery in the northwest.*

THE SOUTHWEST

gorge with a waterfall at the far end. It is located at Adeje, just 6km (4 miles) from Playa de las Américas.

Another popular excursion in the area is to the remote village of **Masca**, set in beautiful mountain scenery in the north of the region. Here, outdoor enthusiasts can enjoy a walk down the Masca gorge to the coast. Few visitors to the southwest of the island leave without an excursion to the **Mount Teide National Park**, which is easily reached from the coastal resorts.

COSTA DEL SILENCIO

The Silent Coast, which is something of a misnomer, is the name given to the area between Los Cristianos and Reina Sofia Airport. Although this stretch of coastline may once have been quiet, today it is beset with the noise of screeching jets and the throb of music from the bars and discos of a number of modest little resorts. Despite the development, it is not a particularly attractive shoreline being hemmed in by banana plantations covered with plastic sacking. Most of the narrow beaches are of black volcanic shingle interspersed with low cliffs and headlands.

South of the airport, the first settlement reached is the fishing village of **Los Abrigos**. So far, it has largely resisted development, but has a handful of cheap seafood restaurants that attract visitors. West of Los Abrigos are two of Tenerife's best golf courses, namely

Golf del Sur (tel: 922 73 81 70; website: www.golfdelsur.net) and the **Amarilla Golf and Country Club** (tel: 922 73 03 19; website: www.amarillagolf.es). The former is generally reckoned to be the most exclusive club on the island, and although it welcomes visitors, they must show proof of their handicap. Golf de Sur has 27 holes, a deep barranco as a major hazard and bunkers of black volcanic sand. Amarilla is an 18-hole golf course and in addition has a nine-hole

▲ *Above: Bus services link the resorts with theme parks and other attractions.*

approach course. It also welcomes visiting golfers.

To the west of the two golf courses is the small resort development of **Costa del Silencio**, which gives this stretch of coastline its name. Adjoining Costa del Silencio is the purpose-built resort of **Ten-Bel**, which is today looking a little dated. It was constructed by Belgian developers, hence its rather unoriginal name. The two resorts consist of the usual collection of hotels, low-rise apartment blocks and villas separated by subtropical gardens and sports facilities. Because the beaches along this coastline are narrow and shingly, a number of sea-water swimming pools have been developed. Water sports on offer include windsurfing and sailing. A yellow submarine, the Finnish-built *Subtrek*, provides regular trips to see the abundant marine life of the nearby Atlantic sea bed; website: www.submarinesafaris.com

The final settlement along the Costa del Silencio is the attractive fishing village of **Las Galletas**. It has benefited from the proximity of Ten-Bel, many of whose visitors make use of the numerous seafood restaurants in the village. Las Galletas has a small seafront promenade lined with shops and cafés. It is gradually spreading out into the surrounding banana plantations, where you will find *Camping Nauta*, Tenerife's largest camping and caravan site.

FERAL EXOTIC BIRDS

Although Tenerife has only a small number of breeding bird species, this is compensated by an interesting exotic blend. Considering the number of theme parks that have large collections of foreign birds, it is inevitable that some of these escape. Some parks, in fact, encourage some of their species to be free-flying. The escapees find that in the benign climate of the Canary Islands they can find plenty of food; many even breed. **Parrots**, **parakeets** and **lovebirds** do particularly well, and flocks of ring-necked parakeets screeching over the apartment blocks are a common sight. Even cage birds such as **zebra finches** (normally resident on the Indian subcontinent) can be seen living in the wild.

THE SOUTHWEST

▲ *Above: The crowded beach between Los Cristianos and Playa de las Américas.*

LOS CRISTIANOS

Popular with package tourists, Los Cristianos was once merely a small fishing port and its boats still supply seafood for much of the southern part of the island. The **harbour** is still the focus of life in the town. The highlight of the day is the arrival and departure of the ferries. Both Fred Olsen and Naviera Armas run car ferries several times a day between Los Cristianos and San Sebastián on La Gomera (note that tickets are not interchangeable between the two lines). In addition, Fred Olsen operates a high-speed hydrofoil on the route. Some of the ferries go on to the islands of La Palma and El Hierro. The harbour at Los Cristianos buzzes with other water activities. Pleasure boats take visitors to watch whales and dolphins, ocean going yachts wait for good conditions to cross the Atlantic, 'Pirate Ships' take the intrepid along the coast for boozy voyages and a host of other small craft bob at their moorings. Deep-sea fishing excursions can also be booked in the kiosks along the harbour wall and marlin, shark and tuna can be guaranteed. Next to the harbour is a well-kept yellow sand beach, which is lined with chair beds and parasols during the summer months. To the north across the harbour road is the even more impressive **Playa de las Vistas**, with an offshore fountain and a promenade which stretches all the way to Playa de las Américas. Both beaches are lined with cafés, bars and restaurants, many serving excellent seafood. The southern end of the beach is the site of a weekly **flea market**, which attracts tourists by the coachload from many parts of the south of the island. Away from the beach, life revolves around the **Plaza del Carmen**, with its pretty modern church. Leading from the main square are a number of traffic-free alleyways full of attractive shops, many selling duty-free goods and traditional craft specialities. In the suburbs of Los Cristianos, rank upon rank of hotels and

LOOKY LOOKY

Tourists at resorts around the east find the shops come to them in the form of street vendors known locally as the 'looky looky boys'. If you sit at a bar along the rambla or beachfront you are sure to catch their eye. They offer a range of items from fake designer items (sunglasses, bags etc) and dvds to carved crafts and mass produced jewellery, all at bargain prices but of varying quality. Some tourists find their approaches a nuisance but a firm no should result in their moving on to the next possible customers.

apartment blocks stretch up into the surrounding hills. Some of those constructed in the early years of development have all the charm of multistorey car parks, but thankfully those designed more recently have more architectural merit.

A DAY TRIP TO LA GOMERA

For visitors staying in the south of Tenerife, there is the possibility of taking a day trip to the island of **La Gomera**, which now has an airport with daily flights from Tenerife Sur to Playa de Santiago. However, many visitors based in the south of the island will still prefer to take the more leisurely ferry. Many local travel agents offer excursions and it is also possible to take a hire car on the ferry and take an independent tour of the island. The voyage to La Gomera (which can be clearly seen from Los Cristianos on most days) takes an hour and a half and there is always the possibility of seeing dolphins and even pilot whales from the boat. If time is at a premium, take Fred Olsen's high-speed hydrofoil, which takes a mere 50 minutes. If the early morning ferry is used, then a stay of eight hours can be enjoyed allowing time to see the best scenic areas on the island. The ferries dock at **San Sebastián de la Gomera**, the main port and capital of the island. This is where Christopher Columbus stopped on his first three voyages across the Atlantic. The object was to take on supplies of water and fresh food, but he also had a romantic interest in a widow, Beatriz de Bobadilla, who was a resident in the town. By the time of his fourth voyage, however, Beatriz had married the formidable Alonso de Lugo, and Columbus wisely took on supplies elsewhere.

La Gomera is one of the smaller Canary Islands, covering about 378km² (146 sq miles). Its landscape is very different from that of

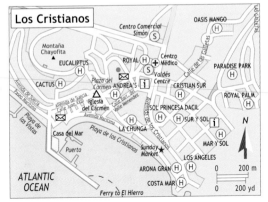

Useful Volcanic Cinders

The rock materials from the volcanoes of Tenerife have been fully utilized by the inhabitants of the island from the time of the Guanches to the present day. Weathered down volcanic ash makes a very fertile soil, while the hard basalt is an excellent building stone. More unusually, volcanic cinders make a useful mulch material on flower beds and in market gardens. The cinders trap moisture from mist in the central cloud layer and at the same time prevent moisture loss from evaporation in sunny weather. In addition, the cinders help to prevent the growth of weeds.

▼ *Below: Tourist development on La Gomera is generally low key.*

Tenerife. There is a frequent cloud cover over the island, so that it is well vegetated, with a dense forest cover in places, and Canary palms common in the lower lying regions. Try to visit the centre of the island, which is the location of the **Parque Nacional de Garajonay** (one of only fifteen such parks in Spain). The highest point on the island is **Mount Garajonay** in the centre of the park, which rises to 1487m (4879ft). The dense forest cover, however, means that there are few views to enjoy. Garajonay covers some 4000ha (9884 acres) with crags, barrancos and steep slopes. With some 600mm (24in) of rain annually, the park has permanently flowing streams, unlike most of the other Canary Islands. This has resulted in large spreads of cloud forest, including unique remnants of *laurissilva* – dark damp areas dominated by the Canarian laurel (*Laurus canariensis*) and tree heath. The main information centre for Garajonay National Park is at Juego de Bolas, near Las Rosas (tel: 922 80 09 93, open daily, 09:30–16:30). As well as information about the Park there is a small garden showing some of the island's main flora. Local crafts such as basketry, pottery and weaving are often demonstrated. The park's information centre is also the start of a number of well-marked walks.

The other scenic feature of La Gomera, not to be missed, is the **Valle Gran Rey** (Valley of the Great King). It was discovered in the 1970s by hippies wanting an alternative lifestyle, putting La Gomera on the tourist map for the first time. Valle Gran Rey is a beautiful steep-sided valley, clothed with terraces growing bananas, papayas and many other subtropical crops.

Don't expect much tourist activity in La Gomera – people come here for the

tranquillity! The only resort of any size is **Playa de Santiago** in the south of the island. This is the location of the airport which opened in 2001. The Fred Olsen company have built a hotel complex and there are a few beaches – but don't get too excited, as they are generally narrow and composed of black sand or shingle. Don't look for any volcanic features either. Though the island is largely composed of volcanic rock, there has been no activity for millions of years. If taking a car over to La Gomera, be aware that the roads are narrow and winding. Although the island is small, journeys can take longer than expected.

Tour operators' excursions visit the aforementioned features and the trips usually include a demonstration of the local whistling 'language', which has been handed down from the times of the Guanches (*see* panel, page 91).

PLAYA DE LAS AMÉRICAS

Up until the early 1960s this stretch of coast was a stony, arid area of semi-desert, relieved only by a few banana plantations. Then the developers moved in and created an entirely artificial holiday resort. Opinions about Playa de las Américas vary. Its detractors emphasize the noisy nightlife, with clubs, bars, discos and pubs unashamedly designed to appeal to the younger set. With English pubs, German beer gardens and international food, it could be said that you would be hard pushed to know you were actually in Spain. On the other hand, it is a well-planned resort with tree-lined avenues and imaginatively designed apartment blocks and hotels. Most of the hotels in Playa de las Américas have facilities like swimming pools and tennis courts, while their grounds are full of sub-tropical plants – like miniature botanic gardens. One hotel, the Bahia del Duque, which is in the form of a Canarian village, is probably the most luxurious on the island.

Interspersed with the hotels and apartments are commercial centres. **Safari Centre** opposite the Mare Nostrum hotel is the best, with specialist and designer shops. **Santiago III** is a multistorey shopping centre amid an apartment complex of the same name. **City Center**, near La Siesta hotel, has some

RENEWABLE ENERGY

Tenerife has plenty of sun and wind and inevitably there has been keen interest in renewable forms of energy. It is now standard for new houses and industrial premises to have solar power. Modern wind 'farms' are also appearing in many parts of the island along with sea and wave power experiments. To see how renewable energy is developing in Tenerife, head for Granadilla in the south of the island where you will find the **Institute of Technology and Renewable Energy**. Here, an outdoor technological walkway takes you through the latest advances.

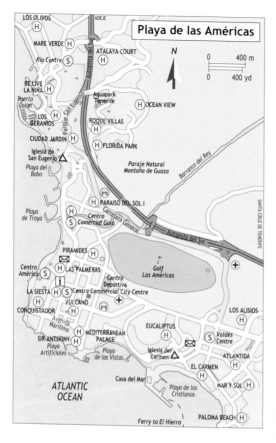

Playa de las Américas

LOS OLIVOS (H)
ADEJE
MARE VERDE (H)
ATALAYA COURT (H)
Rio Centre (S)
Autopista del Sur
BE LIVE LA NIÑA (H)
Puerto Colón
Aquapark Tenerife
Parque San Eugenio
OCEAN VIEW (H)
LOS GERANIOS (H)
ROQUE VILLAS (H)
CIUDAD JARDIN (H)
FLORIDA PARK (H)
Iglesia de San Eugenio △
Playa del Bobo
Paraje Natural Montaña de Guaza
Barranco del Rey
SANTA CRUZ DE TENERIFE
PARAISO DEL SOL I (H)
Playa de Troya
Centro Comercial Gala (S) (H)
Carretera general
Autopista del Sur
PIRAMIDES (H)
Golf Las Americas
Centro América (S)
LAS PALMERAS (H)
Centro Deportivo
LA SIESTA (H)(S)
Centro Comercial City Centre
VULCANO (H)
CONQUISTADOR (H)
LOS ALISIOS (H)
Avenida Marítima
EUCALIPTUS (H)
Valdés Centre (S)
SIR ANTHONY (H)
MEDITERRANEAN PALACE (H)
Playa Artificiales
Playa de las Vistas
Iglesia del Carmen △
ATLANTIDA (H)
Casa del Mar
EL CARMEN (H)
ATLANTIC OCEAN
Playa de los Cristianos
MAR Y SOL (H)
Ferry to El Hierro
PALOMA BEACH (H)

N

0   400 m
0   400 yd

good specialist shops with duty-free goods. **Shopping Center Oasis** also has some high-quality shops. At night, Commercial Centres change their character completely as discos and night clubs open their doors and music throbs, often until daybreak. Playa de las Américas has three small, well-kept **beaches** – Playa del Bobo, Playa de Troya and Playa Colón – with rows of sun beds and parasols; they can get very crowded during the height of the season. Backing the beaches is a tree-lined promenade, and it is now possible to walk to Los Cristianos. Perhaps the most pleasant part of the resort is **Puerto Colón**, a luxurious marina crammed with yachts and backed by chandlers' shops, restaurants and bars. A statue of Columbus points across the sea towards America. Boats and pedaloes can be hired at the marina.

Above all, Playa de las Américas is an all-action resort. In addition to its nightlife, there is a wide range of activities available, such as go-karting, paragliding, water-skiing, sailing, deep-sea fishing, dolphin-watching, windsurfing, diving, jeep safaris and countless others. Make sure that both you and the operators are insured for these adventure activities. Just outside the resort are two of the best golf courses on the island. **Golf Las Américas** (tel: 922 75 20 05; website: www.golflamericas. com) is an 18-hole course designed by John Jacobs close to

WATER SPORTS

The resorts in southwest Tenerife offer all kinds of water sports, ranging from pedaloes, banana boats, parasailing and jet skis to sailing, scuba diving, windsurfing and water-skiing. Swimmers should beware of underwater rocks and strong currents.

exit 28 of the motorway. It has a restaurant and driving range. **Golf Costa Adeje** (tel: 922 71 00 00; website: www.golf costaadeje.com) is near the end of the motorway. It has 18 holes with a further nine holes now available. Buggies and clubs can be hired at both courses and visitors are welcomed. A quartet of **theme parks** plus a zoo are within easy reach and free shuttle buses link them with the main hotels. Certainly, no visitor to Playa de las Américas could complain of boredom!

THEME PARKS

When the sun and sand pall or the weather is cloudy, visitors (especially those with children) can choose from a number of easily reached theme parks for diversion.

Jungle Park ★★★

This park opened in 1994 and has proved extremely popular with visitors. Originally it concentrated on displays of free-flying birds of prey, but now there are penguins, dolphins, crocodiles, flamingos and elephants, plus some rides for children – all set in nearly 8ha (20 acres) of beautifully landscaped grounds complete with waterfalls and lakes. The main criticism against the park has been that few of its animals are in fact native to Tenerife, but this does not seem to worry the majority of its visitors intent on a great day out. The park is 3km (2 miles) from Los Cristianos on the Arona road. Leave the motorway at Junction 27. It is open daily, 10:00–17:30; tel: 922 72 90 10; website: www.aguilas junglepark.com There is an admission charge.

Aqualand ★

This waterpark makes an excellent alternative to the beaches and will be particularly appreciated by younger

JEEP SAFARIS

A good way of exploring the Tenerife countryside is by going on a jeep safari. These four-wheel-drive off-road vehicles can reach parts of the countryside such as forest trails and rough volcanic terrain, which are out of bounds to normal cars. But remember that open-top jeep safaris can be hot, windy and uncomfortable. On these trips, don't expect much in the way of wildlife as Tenerife has few mammals and only a small number of bird species. The scenery, however, will be magnificent and the emphasis will be on having a good time. Choose a reputable company with reliable vehicles.

▼ *Below: A meal with a view at a beachside restaurant in Playa de las Américas.*

▼ *Below: The local aquapark is popular with children and adults.*

visitors. There are numerous pools, water slides, shutes, fountains and simulated waves, all set in attractively land-scaped grounds. There is also a large dolphinarium and these aquatic mammals appear in regular shows. The aquapark is located next to the motorway at San Eugenio Alto, Playa de las Américas. Leave the motorway at Junction 29 and follow the signs. It is open July–August daily 10:00–18:00, rest of year daily 10:00–17:00; tel: 922 71 52 66; website: www. aqualand.es Admission charge.

Monkey Park ★

Founded in 1991, this is one of the most unusual mass-appeal attractions on the island, being part zoological garden/part centre for protection of endangered species. As the name suggests, the main draw are the monkeys and primates with a wide range in all sizes from marmosets to chimps. All are housed in environments mimicking as closely as possible their natural homelands around the world. Monkey Park is also at the forefront of the fight to improve the numbers of endangered primates in captivity in order to try to create a viable breeding population. It's a great educational centre with lots of information about primates, their habitats and their lifestyles, but the

best part for adults and children alike is to get close to these cute creatures – some of which are our closest genetic relatives. If you tire of monkeys, the park has other animal attractions including collections of birds and reptiles. This attraction (website: www.monkeypark.com) is open daily, 09:30–17:00, tel: 922 79 07 21. Admission charge. To reach Monkey Park, leave the motorway at Junction 26.

Aloe Park ★★

For those visitors staying in the south of the island this working banana and aloe plantation makes a good day out. Visits are by guided tours which take place at intervals throughout the day. The first stop is a talk with visual displays about the production of bananas (and other tropical fruit), with a particularly interesting account of how crops in the lowland are irrigated with rain that falls on Mount Teide. The tour then goes into the plastic-covered banana plantations and on to a museum of farming tools and machinery plus a petting zoo of traditional farm animals. The gift shop sells banana recipe books, seeds and banana liqueur, while there are, predictably, plenty of banana-based desserts in the restaurant. Open Monday–Friday 09:00–16:30. Guided tours take place at 10:00, 11:30, 13:00, 15:30 and 16:15; tel: 922 72 03 60. Leave the motorway at Junction 26 and then follow the signs.

Siam Park ★★

One of the largest water parks in Europe, Siam Park is the newest must-visit attraction on Tenerife and has been a massive hit with exceptional approval ratings on social media. Styled like an old Siamese city the park is packed with adrenaline fuelled rides, chutes and a surf pool, plus a range of gentler watery activities for families with younger children. There's a Thai-style marketplace selling a whole range of souvenirs. To reach the park, take junction 26 off the motorway (tel: 902 06 00 00; website: www.siampark.net) Open May–Oct daily 10:00–18:00, Nov–Apr daily 10:00–17:00. There's an admission charge and a combined ticket price with Loro Parque. All

THE WILD CANARY

The bright yellow canary trilling in its cage is familiar to everybody and will often be seen in Tenerife. Its wild ancestor, however, is a much different bird. The canary (*Serinus canaria*) is endemic to Madeira, the Azores and the Canary Islands. In the wild it is quite a drab bird, with striated markings and only a touch of dull yellow-green. It can be seen in a variety of habitats, but usually near pine forests (where it builds its nest) and cultivated fields. Only the male sings and its trilling bears little resemblance to the virtuoso performance of the captive bird.

THE SOUTHWEST

▶ *Right: The cliffs of Los Gigantes reach a height of over 600m (1970ft).*

WHALE-WATCHING

The harbour at Los Cristianos is a good place to book a boat trip to watch whales and dolphins. Some of the boats have underwater viewing to watch these magnificent creatures. Whale-watching has become so popular that there are now regulations that limit the number of boats taking part in the activity. One of the world's most important colonies of **short-finned pilot whales** (*Ballenas pilotos*) are regularly seen off the southwest coast of Tenerife. They can weigh more than 3000kg (6615lb) and reach up to 5m (16ft) in length. At migration time a number of other species may be seen including **sperm whales** (*Physeter macrocephalus*). Dolphins are relatively common off the waters of Tenerife and include the **common dolphin** (*Delphinus delphis*) and the **bottlenose dolphin** (*Tursiops truncates*). Both are frequently seen swimming and jumping alongside boats. Regrettably, few of the boats have naturalists on board to explain the behaviour of these fascinating marine mammals.

the theme parks can be reached by **free shuttle bus** from the main resorts. The brochures in the tourist office show the pick-up places and times, or consult the websites of the individual attractions.

NORTH FROM PLAYA DE LAS AMÉRICAS

Las Americas merges imperceptibly northwards into the developing resort of **Costa Adeje**, which is typified by self-contained luxury hotels and high class shopping and golf facilities. For the next 20km (12 miles), the coastline, which was once undeveloped, except for a few small fishing villages, is the next target for the developers. Already there are a number of small self-contained resorts with up-market hotels and apartments of futuristic design. In turn, **Callao Salvaje**, **La Caleta** and **Playa Paraíso** are already up and running and sometime in the near future one can envisage them linking up with the Los Cristianos/Playa de la Americas conurbation. Further north, the attractive fishing villages of **San Juán** and **Alcalá** have so far resisted too much development. The former has a busy fishing fleet, a dry dock and a boat-building yard. Watching the morning catch being unloaded is a popular activity. Several boats operate from the harbour at San Juan offering trips to view the cliffs at Los Gigantes, and a launch that runs whale and dolphin watching excursions. Inland from these coastal settlements are long stretches of irrigated tomato and banana plantations, while out to sea on a clear day are impressive views of the island of La Gomera.

PUERTO DE SANTIAGO

Once a small fishing village, Puerto de Santiago is now a grow-ing, up-market tourist resort. The shoreline is mainly rocky, except for the **Playa de la Arena**, a small but clean beach of black volcanic sand which regularly receives the Blue Flag status awarded to the best kept beaches worldwide. A few fishing boats still operate from the town, but many of the fishermen make a more profitable living from taking tourists out on boat trips. Behind the beach, tasteful villas, hotels and apartments suggest that this area does not seek to appeal to the mass tourism of the resorts further south. Northwards, Puerto de Santiago merges into its satellite resort of **Los Gigantes** (the giants), another up-market resort, named after the towering cliffs of black volcanic basalt. Reaching over 600m (1970ft) in height, the cliffs stretch for more than 10km (6 miles). Boat trips to see the cliffs run from the Puerto Deportivo (sport harbour) at Los Gigantes. Other boats leave for scuba diving, dolphin watching or game fish-ing. Some of the boats are glass bottomed. Ocean Explorer (tel: 687 39 58 56, www.ocean-explorer.net) offers whale and dolphin watching from small boats, plus a range of other water-sports activities. There is a small beach of black vol-canic sand, nestling against the cliffs, that is gently sloping and safe for children.

INLAND FROM THE COASTAL RESORTS

Inland, there are few places of inter-est. An exception is the market town of **Adeje**, which has a long history. This was a Guanche regional capital and after the Spanish Conquest it became the power base of the Ponte family, who had originated in Genoa. In the 16th century, they built a fortified residence, the **Casa Fuerte**, which eventually became a centre for the collection of sugar cane

▼ Below: The market town of Adeje is the starting point for walks along the Barranco del Infierno.

THE SOUTHWEST

produced by slave labour. It was partly destroyed by fire in the 19th century and was later used as a storehouse for local tomatoes and bananas. There are now plans to turn the Casa Fuerte into a museum. The only other building of interest in Adeje is the **Iglesia de Santa Ursula**, the parish church dating from the 17th century. It has two aisles, a fine coffered ceiling and a Mexican-style bell tower. Inside, you can see a balcony with a wrought iron screen behind which the Ponte family could worship safe from the inquisitive eyes of the local inhabitants. Look, too, for the statue of the *Virgen del Rosario*, attributed to one of Tenerife's best-known sculptors, Fernando Estévez. Most people come to Adeje, however, to hike into the **Barranco del Infierno** – a steep-sided ravine through which a stream runs for much of the year. The 'Valley of Hell' got its name during the Civil War, when it was the site of numerous executions. The Barranco is reached via the road at the side of the Casa Fuerte. This road, incidentally, has a slope steeper than anything likely to be encountered in the ravine. The path that runs through the Barranco is fairly level and crosses and re-crosses the stream several times before reaching a waterfall (which can be quite impressive in the winter). Beneath the waterfall is a plunge pool. Initially arid, the vegetation becomes more luxuriant as the path proceeds into the gorge. Look out on the higher slopes for old Guanche caves, where several mummies have been discovered. Allow three hours for the return walk and make sure you have strong footwear. The local authority, recognising the fragility of the environment, now limit walkers to 200 on any one day and charge an entrance fee. Swimming in the plunge pool is banned. The Bar-Restaurant Otelo, at the entrance to the Barranco, will be difficult to resist at the end of the hike. Those people arriving by car may find parking difficult, so arrive early. The barranco is currently closed to allow for improvements to the footpath.

▼ *Below: One of the best hikes in Tenerife is along the picture-perfect Barranco del Infierno.*

Further north is the market town of **Guía de Isora**. Although recent volcanic lava comes quite close to the town, it is surrounded by fertile soil growing potatoes and tomatoes, while almond blossoms make a stunning sight in the early spring. The parish church of the Virgen de la Luz, is worth a quick visit to see the Artonesado ceiling and the statues by José Luján Pérez.

After the village of **Tamaimo**, the road climbs steeply through hairpin bends to **Santiago del Teide**, which lies in the pass between the Teno Mountains to the west and the Mount Teide volcanic area to the east. Santiago has a pleasant, wide, tree-lined main street with one or two restaurants and a bodega where you can taste the wines that are grown in the area. The Moorish-looking 20th-century church is of interest, with its whitewashed walls and dome. Two minor roads lead away from Santiago del Teide. One leads south to the village of **Arguayo**, close to the lava that dates from the island's last eruption in 1909. There has been a revival in Guanche-style pottery making in the village. The other road leads northwest into the Teno Hills to the pass known as the **Degollada de Cherfe**. From here there are probably the best vistas on the island, with the majestic Teide to the east, the deep valley of the Teno Mountains to the north and away to the west the islands of La Gomera and La Palma. Proceeding over the pass, the road drops down in a series of hairpin bends to the village of **Masca**. Once remote and only accessible by donkey, this pretty village now attracts the tour coaches by the score. An enterprising mayor had the road built, brought water and electricity to the village and set up a small museum (reached via a steep path). Visitors driving hire cars here should be aware that, despite the improved road, the numerous hairpin bends ensure a nerve-racking drive. The tourist trade does not seem to have ruined Masca, even though a small number of bars, restaurants and gift shops have appeared. The village is also a good centre for hiking. The best walk is down the **Barranco de Masca** to the sea, a distance of around 8km (5 miles) with stupendous views all the way and some varied flora to appreciate. Allow two hours for the walk and arrange for a boat from Los Gigantes to pick you up in order to avoid having to return uphill to Masca.

SORTING OUT YOUR CAMELS

Many visitors to Tenerife are tempted to try camel riding. As an example, there are opportunities at El Tanque and Los Cristianos Zoo, where riders can be dressed up in Arab clothes for the experience. However, the beast that they will ride is actually a dromedary. The **Bactrian Camel** (*Camelus bactrianus*) has two humps, while the camel which is seen in Tenerife is in fact the **Arabian Camel** (*Camelus dromedaries*) or **Dromedary**. These are large animals – standing up to 2m (6.5ft) tall – and their colours vary from brown through fawn to almost white. Camels and dromedaries make excellent beasts of burden as they have large storage pockets for water in their stomachs and food reserves in their humps, while they can carry many times their own weight. Tenerife's dromedaries were originally imported from North Africa and today they still have Moroccan handlers.

THE SOUTHWEST AT A GLANCE

BEST TIMES TO VISIT

The sunny climate of the southwest makes it an all-year-round destination. It is particularly popular in winter, however, as it is the nearest area to Northern Europe that has guaranteed warm sun at this time of the year. Expect crowds at all seasons. Wild flowers on the lower slopes of the hills are superb in spring.

GETTING THERE

The southwest of Tenerife is easily reached from Reina Sofía Airport (Tenerife Sur), using the motorway. A trip in a **car** that was hired at the airport, for example, would take approximately 20 minutes to reach Los Cristianos and approximately 50 minutes to reach Los Gigantes. **Taxis** can also be hired at the airport. TITSA **buses** (www.titsa. com) call at the airport en route from Santa Cruz to Los Cristianos and other resorts so they are also available as an option.

GETTING AROUND

The **motorway**, TF1, runs to the northeast of both Los Cristianos and Playa de las Américas. The other **roads** form a network in the coastal area, but relatively few of the minor roads penetrate any distance inland. **Buses** run by the TITSA company link the main settlements, while free shuttle buses connect the resorts to the theme parks. **Taxis** are cheap and plentiful.

WHERE TO STAY

A vast selection is available in the main resorts. Many hotels and apartments run to full capacity all year and are pre-booked by tour companies. Visitors who don't book ahead may find it difficult to get accommodation.

Luxury

Hotel Gran Bahia del Duque, Playa del Duque, Fanabe, tel: 922 74 69 00, fax: 922 74 69 16, www.bahia-duque.com Most luxurious on Tenerife. Beachside, with pools, subtropical grounds and all facilities.

Spring Arona Gran Hotel, Avenida Maritima, Los Cristianos, tel: 922 78 86 83, fax: 922 75 02 43, www. springhoteles.com Modern hotel at the eastern end of Los Cristianos overlooking the beach. Pools and restaurants.

Mediterranean Palace, Avenida la Américas, Playa de las Américas, tel: 922 75 75 45, www.marenostrumresort. com Large hotel with excellent facilities.

Mid-range

Sol Princesa Dacil, Calle Penetración, Los Cristianos, tel: 922 75 30 30, fax: 922 79 06 58, www.melia.com A few minutes from harbour.

Hotel Stil Los Gigantes, Calle Flor de Pascua 12, Los Gigantes, tel: 922 86 10 20, fax: 922 86 04 75, www. stilhotels.com Modern hotel with pools and fitness centre.

H10 Conquistador, Avenida Rafael Puig 36, Playa de las Américas, tel: 922 75 30 00, www.h10hotels.com Good facilities, health and beauty centre.

Budget

Pension la Paloma, Calle Peatonal Berlin 7, Los Cristianos, tel: 922 79 01 98. Family-run, near harbour.

Andrea's Hotel, Avenida Valle Menendez 6, Los Cristianos, tel: 922 79 00 12, fax: 922 79 42 70, www.hotelesreveron.com Commercial hotel in a modern block. Convenient overnight stay for the morning ferry to La Gomera.

La Gomera

Visitors on an excursion to La Gomera might want to stay.

Luxury

Parador de la Gomera, Balcón de la Villa y Puerto, tel: 922 87 11 00, fax: 922 87 11 16. Set in colonial-style mansion; one of the best paradors in the chain. Booking: www.parador.es

Mid-range

Hotel Villa Gomera, Ruiz de Padrón 68, San Sebastián, tel: 922 87 00 20, fax: 922 87 02 35, www.hotelvillagomera.com Small hotel in the centre of town.

Budget

Casa Humberto, Valle Gran Rey, tel: 922 80 54 51, www. apartmentoscasahumberto. com Inexpensive studios and apartments set on a hillside.

WHERE TO EAT

Visitors to the main resorts are swamped with choice when

it comes to restaurants, from simple Canarian food to international menus and exotic far eastern establishments. There are prices to suit all pockets.

Luxury
Molino Blanco, Avenida de Austria 5, San Eugenio Alto, tel: 922 79 62 82, www.molino-blanco.com Fine dining in a beautifully converted windmill.
Oliver's with a Twist, Calle Hermano Pedro de Bethancourt, Los Cristianos, tel: 680 69 39 77. Excellent British cuisine served with contemporary flair.

Mid-range
Otelo, Calle los Molinos 44, Barranco del Infierno, Adeje, tel: 922 78 03 74. Popular Canarian restaurant situated at the entrance to the gorge. It serves good rabbit dishes.
Doña Juana, Playa Azul, Playa de las Américas, tel: 922 79 66 53. Excellent Canarian cuisine, specializing in seafood.
Casa del Mar, Esplanada del Muelle, Los Cristianos, tel: 922 76 13 23. This award-winning seafood restaurant is situated close to the harbour.
El Rincon de Juan Carlos, Pasaje de Jacaranda 2, Los Gigantes, tel: 922 86 80 40, www.elrincondejuancarlos.es This young internationally trained chef is back in his homeland with a creative Spanish menu.

Budget
Pailebot, Promenade, Los

Cristianos, tel: 922 79 18 61. Cheap Canarian food with friendly service. There are a number of reasonably priced Indian and Chinese restaurants in the main resorts. Try **Bombay Babu**, Torviscas Playa, tel: 922 71 94 63, www.bombay-babu.com There are also a host of cheap pizzerias, many with take-away services. *Tapas* bars are more likely to be found in Los Cristianos. Try **The Willows**, Centro Comercial Apolo, Calle Hermano Pedro Bethancourt, Los Cristianos, tel: 922 97 26 19, www.thewillowstenerife.wix.com Great choice of *tapas*.

La Gomera
Junonia, Avda Maritima, Playa de Santiago, tel: 922 89 57 61. Pretty restaurant overlooking the harbour. Fish a speciality.

TOURS AND EXCURSIONS
Boat trips are popular from Los Cristianos for whale and dolphin watching. *Shogun* and *Peter Pan* (both tel: 922 79 80 44, www.barcostenerife.com) are old wooden sailing ships. Trips can be booked at the harbourside kiosks, where sport fishing can also be arranged. From Los Gigantes, Nashiri Uno and Gladiator U offer trips (tel: 922 86 19 18, www.maritimaacantilados.com) A day trip by ferry to **La Gomera** is another possibility. The numerous **theme parks** close to the resort can be accessed using the free shuttle buses. **Jeep safaris** can be booked at most hotel desks.

The most popular **coach excursions** are a round island trip, visiting Candleria, Puerto de la Cruz, Pueblo Chico, Icod de los Vinos and Los Gigantes; a trip to Mount Teide National Park to see the volcanic features; and a visit to Loro Parque.

USEFUL CONTACTS
Tourist Information Offices:
Costa Adeje – Centro Comercial Plaza del Duque, tel: 922 71 63 77. Open Oct–Jun, Mon–Fri 10:00–17:00; Jul–Sep, Mon–Fri 10:00–16:00.
Playa de Las Américas – Plaza del City Center, Avda Rafael Puig 1, tel: 922 79 76 68. Open Mon–Fri, 09:00–21:00; Sat–Sun 09:00–15:30.

Ferries: Los Cristianos is the ferry port for the three western islands of La Gomera, El Hierro and La Palma.
Lineas Fred Olsen, tel: 902 10 01 07, website: www.fredolsen.es runs several car ferries a day to San Sebastian on La Gomera and daily sailings to El Hierro and La Palma.
Naviera Armas, tel: 922 53 40 50, www.navieraarmas.com operates a number of daily ferries to La Gomera, with the ship going on to La Palma on five days a week.

Disabled travellers: Los Cristianos has a specialist organisation for disabled travellers including hiring out wheelchairs. Contact Le Ro, Avenida Amsterdam 8, tel: 922 75 02 89, www.lero.net

7
Mount Teide National Park

If the visitor to Tenerife has only enough time to make one excursion, it should certainly be to the Mount Teide National Park (or, to be strictly correct, Las Cañadas del Teide National Park). Mount Teide itself dominates the island. At 3718m (12,199ft) it is the highest point on the Canary Islands and indeed the tallest mountain in all of Spain. Its perfect cone shape makes clear its volcanic origins and although it is at present dormant, there are many well-preserved volcanic features to the south of the main peak in the area known as Las Cañadas. (The word *Cañadas* derives from the gravelly plains beneath the main peak.) Las Cañadas del Teide National Park was set up in 1954 and covers an area of 18,990ha (46,925 acres), making it the fifth largest reserve in Spain. The entire park lies at 2000m (6562ft) above sea level.

One of the first recorded ascents of Mount Teide was by the German scientist Alexander von Humboldt in 1799. Today, over 300,000 people climb to the summit annually. The amazing moonlike landscape of Mount Teide and the wonderfully clear air around its summit has led to it becoming a popular location for filming. Films shot here include *The Clash of the Titans* and *One Million Years BC*. Apart from its volcanic features, the park has a wide range of unusual flowers, plus a small number of rare bird species.

Mount Teide is one of fifteen national parks in Spain. Four of these are in the Canary Islands – Mount Teide on Tenerife, the Timanfaya National Park ('Mountains of Fire') on Lanzarote, Caldera de Taburiente, a volcanic crater landscape

ATLANTIC OCEAN
La Laguna
Puerto de la Cruz
SANTA CRUZ DE TENERIFE
La Orotava
Pico del Teide
3718 m
Playa de las Américas
Los Cristianos
ATLANTIC OCEAN

Don't Miss

*** Cable Car to the top of Mount Teide: for superb views of volcanic features, the rest of Tenerife and many of the other Canary Islands.
** The Roques de García: fantastic rock shapes in the centre of the National Park.
** Parador Las Cañadas del Teide: stay the night at this state-run hotel and watch the sun rise and set on snow-capped Mount Teide.
** Las Cañadas Caldera: enjoy the lunar landscape of this huge collapsed crater.

◀ *Opposite: The cable car transports visitors close to the summit of Mount Teide.*

MOUNT TEIDE NATIONAL PARK

▶ *Opposite: A number of the miradors en route to Mount Teide offer quite spectacular views.*

on La Palma, and the Garajonay National Park, a cloud forest reserve, on the island of La Gomera. National parks form the highest level of conservation in Spain, closely followed by natural (or nature) parks, such as the Corralejo Dunes on the island of Fuerteventura.

ROUTES TO TEIDE

There are four main routes leading to Mount Teide National Park and there is much discussion among visitors and tourists alike as to which of these routes ranks highest in terms of scenery. It would probably be advisable to choose the nearest route from the resort where you are staying in order to get there early in the morning before the crowds, and then return by a different route later in the day.

Visitors who are staying in Puerto de la Cruz should preferably take the TF-21 via La Orotava. The winding road has several miradors giving views northwards over the Orotava Valley. At one of these, the **Rosa de Piedra**, there is a rock

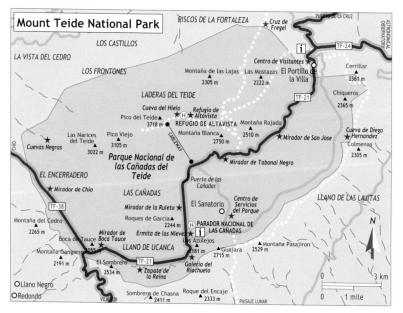

Mount Teide National Park

face with a gigantic structure resembling a stone rose. There
is also a trout farm at Aguamansa and you will pass a stretch
of pine forest before reaching the visitors' centre and the
national park boundary at El Portillo.

The second route, and the longest, runs from Santa Cruz
and La Laguna along the ridge of the Cumbre Dorsal. Around
Esperanza the landscape is mainly farmland and then the
route passes through a long stretch of Canarian pines. Look
out for the monument which marks the spot where General
Franco had an alfresco lunch (believed to be a paella) with
some of his army supporters just a fortnight before the
outbreak of the Spanish Civil War. There are also a number of
miradors on this route giving vistas over both the north and
south coasts. Don't miss the **tarta** – a strange strata of volcanic ash that looks like layers of a cake. Further along, on
the south side of the road, are the white towers of the **Teide
Observatory** run by the Department of Astrophysics at La
Laguna University (*see* panel, page 106). This route joins the
Puerto de la Cruz road at El Portillo.

Visitors staying at the main resorts of Los Cristianos and
Playa de las Américas in the southwest of the island have
a choice of two routes. The most tortuous road leaves the
coast near El Médano and climbs up through Granadilla de
Abona and Vilaflor with hairpin bends flanked by vineyards
and terraces growing tomatoes, potatoes and other crops. It
is worth stopping at the Mirador San Roque where there are

LAVA TYPES

Mount Teide and the surrounding area exhibit many types
of volcanic material, both
liquid and solid. When molten
magma erupts from a volcano,
the eventual form of the lava
depends on a number of factors,
including its chemical composi-
tion and the rate of cooling. The
descriptive names that are given
are often Hawaiian in origin, for
it was in these islands that the
first research was carried out.
Aa (pronounced 'ah-ah') lava
is viscous material that cools
slowly and has a dark, clinker-
like appearance. **Pahoehoe**
(pronounced 'perhoyhoy') lava
is glassier and lighter in colour
and often cools as ropey lava.
Some lava cools in the form of
pillows, probably after contact
with water. **Basalt** is a fluid
black lava that travels for long
distances and cools in hexagonal
columns. It is the most common
volcanic rock on Tenerife.

MOUNT TEIDE NATIONAL PARK

▲ *Above: The distinctive white towers and domes of the Teide Observatory, located to the east of Mount Teide.*

superb views across the terraced hillsides towards the island of La Gomera. Just past Vilaflor, a hiking track leads to the **Paisaje Lunar** or Lunar Landscape – an area of white volcanic ash that has been eroded into pointed columns and other strange shapes. The road continues through pine forests to reach the western end of the national park at Boca de Tauce.

Visitors staying in the more northerly resorts of Los Gigantes and Puerto de Santiago should take the route via Tamaimo and Chío, the road taken by most of the tour coaches. There are spectacular views westward to the islands of La Palma and La Gomera, before the road passes through an expanse of pine forest. The picnic sites here are good spots to see the rare blue chaffinch. On the left-hand side of the road are large stretches of black lava, which date from the eruptions of 1798 and still look very fresh. Shortly afterwards you reach Boca de Tauce, the entrance to the national park. Visitors using public transport should take bus 348 from Puerto de la Cruz.

CLIMATE

Mount Teide National Park is impressive at all times of the year, particularly in **winter**, when the peak is snow-capped. Unfortunately during this season many of the hiking trails may be closed and the cable car may not run because of wind or ice. Late **spring** sees a wealth of wild flowers, including the red *tajinaste* which can reach a height of 2m (6.5ft). Most tourists visit the area in **summer**, when there is less likelihood of cloud, but the facilities may be crowded.

THE WEATHER ON MOUNT TEIDE

It obviously makes perfect sense to visit Mount Teide National Park on a clear day, but Mount Teide is so high that it is frequently above the layer of cloud that forms between approximately 500m (1640ft) and 1500m (4920ft). It is possible that you might emerge from the dense cloud cover into bright sunshine when entering the park. The peak of Mount Teide is often covered in snow during winter, but even at this time of year it is quite possible to get rather badly burnt by the sun in the clear air. Chilly winds at this height are very common, and it is therefore advisable to bring warm clothing whatever the season. Humidity is very low, nearly always below 50 per cent.

GEOLOGICAL HISTORY OF MOUNT TEIDE

The Canary Islands were formed when magma forced its way through the earth's crust creating volcanoes and islands. The earliest of the Canary Islands to be formed in this way were Fuerteventura and Lanzarote in the east. These islands, because of erosion, are low-lying. The most recently formed volcanic islands are in the west and include Tenerife.

There have been numerous volcanic episodes in Tenerife's volcanic history, which probably began between 8 and 12 million years ago. Mount Teide is just the latest in a series of volcanoes to erupt on the island. One of its predecessors is thought

▼ Below: The road through the national park gives excellent views of the area's volcanic features.

MOUNT TEIDE NATIONAL PARK

WALKING IN THE PARK

Keen and fit hikers will want to tackle Mount Teide itself, but for the less energetic there are many less demanding walks. For example, there are two walks that start and finish at the Parador. One is a circular route that goes around the Roques de García covering around 4km (2.5 miles) in about two hours. For the more energetic there is the Montaña Majua route, hiking 11km (7 miles) in approximately four hours. More challenging is the Siete Cañadas route which starts at El Portillo visitors' centre and finishes at the Parador, covering some 15km (9 miles) in around five hours. A number of the walks are led by local guides. For details collect a brochure from the visitors' centre.

to have been nearly 5000m (16,400ft) in height and of a type known as a shield volcano. Its peak eventually collapsed forming a megacrater or **caldera**. This is the giant amphitheatre known today as Las Cañadas. The walls of the caldera are in places 16km (10 miles) apart and the circumference measures 45km (28 miles). Mount Teide has formed within the caldera on its northern edge partly burying the crater wall.

Mount Teide probably started forming around 600,000 years ago. In historical time, Columbus noted that the volcano was smoking when he sailed past on his way to the New World in 1492. There were certainly three eruptions in the 18th century, with a major flow of lava occurring in 1798. The so-called *Las Narices del Teide* (Teide's nostrils), a series of small craters on the mountain's southwestern flank, date from this time. A minor eruption in 1909 was the last significant volcanic event. Teide is dormant at present, but experts suggest that the volcano is far from extinct.

THE FEATURES OF THE NATIONAL PARK

Visitors entering the national park from the resorts in the west will arrive at **Boca de Tauce**, where there is a notice board showing a diagram of the view towards Mount Teide. The different types of lava flow can be seen clearly here, while to the right is the first of the *cañadas*, the **Llano de Ucanca**, which may mark the bed of an old crater lake.

▶ ▶ *Opposite: One of the graphic displays at Mount Teide National Park's visitors' centre.*
▶ *Right: The peak of Mount Teide with Los Roques in the foreground.*

Centro de Visitantes ★★

In many ways, however, it is better to enter the park from the east, because where the roads from La Orotava and La Laguna meet, at El Portillo, is the **Centro de Visitantes**. The visitors' centre is open 09:00–16:00 and it is well worth spending some time looking at the numerous displays and models to get your bearings and locate the main features of the park.

The centre is accessed through a mock-up of a lava tube (a cave which is formed within moving lava) complete with the roars of volcanic eruptions. There is an audio room here, which provides a short video programme that is shown at regular intervals in a variety of languages, dealing with the national parks of the Canary Islands in general and Mount Teide in particular. There is also a bookshop where you can buy brochures and other publications outlining the park's flora and fauna. The visitors' centre can also provide useful information about the numerous walking trails within the park – it is essential to call here before walking in the winter

A CHILD-FRIENDLY ISLAND

Do not worry about taking babies or young children to Tenerife, as they will be made very welcome. Spanish children keep late nights and are not excluded from any family activities. Waiters traditionally make a huge fuss of small children who come to their restaurants and will prepare special portions for them. Older children will find plenty to occupy them from sandy beaches to theme parks and boat trips.

MOUNT TEIDE NATIONAL PARK

months as some of the routes may be closed in bad weather. You can either walk independently or join one of the guided walking tours organized by the centre.

Before leaving the centre, do visit the 'Botanical Gardens', where paths meander among a collection of the plants and flowers that grow in the National Park. Some of these plants are threatened by the introduction of grazing animals such as rabbits and moufflon, whose numbers are now controlled. There is a small nursery where these rare plants are being propagated. The gardens are a good place to see some of the typical wildlife of the National Park. There are scores of Canarian lizards and butterflies such as monarchs and painted ladies can be spotted at the right season. There are several restaurants clustered around the Visitors' Centre, providing an excellent opportunity for a lunch stop.

The road from El Portillo runs westwards through the heart of the national park. To the left are three volcanic peaks – **Las Mostazas**, **Montaña Rajada** and **Montaña Blanca**. The latter is the starting point for a number of treks to the top of Mount Teide. All around the area here are wide stretches of yellow and red volcanic ash, interspersed with

COLOURFUL VOLCANIC ROCKS

Visitors to the Mount Teide National Park are often fascinated by the variety of colours in the volcanic rocks, particularly in the area known as Los Azulejos, which is named after the brightly coloured Spanish tiles. Generally speaking volcanic material becomes lighter in colour with age. Many of the darker lavas are full of **obsidian**, a black glassy mineral that has cooled quickly before crystal structures have had time to form. The lighter coloured gravelly materials are usually composed of **pumice**. Other rocks owe their colours to their **mineral content**, iron staining the rocks brown and red, while copper produces green and blue tints.

the occasional layer of black obsidian, which the Guanches used as a cutting tool. To the left of the road is the area known as **Arenas Blancas** (which means 'White Sands'), with its dunes of gravelly pumice resembling a desert.

Cable Car ★★★

Shortly, on the right-hand (north) side of the road, is the **Cable Car Station**. Two small gondolas operate at a time, taking only eight minutes to transport visitors to **La Rambleta**, which is just 170m (558ft) below the summit of Mount Teide. To walk the last 170m to the summit requires a permit, obtainable from the National Park office (www.reservasparquesnacionales.es). Permits are limited to 150 per day, and applicants will need to show their passports. The crater itself is very dangerous and out of bounds to visitors.

There are two additional signposted paths – one goes westward past a number of fumeroles belching sulphurous smoke and gives a good view of **Pico Viejo**, at a height of 3105m (10,188ft), as well as its impressive crater which is approximately 800m (2625ft) in diameter. The other path runs in an easterly direction to a mirador passing some superb tongues of lava en route.

◄ *Opposite: Layers of pumice, ash and lava exposed at the roadside.*
▼ *Below: Views from the upper station of the cable car are the best in the Canary Islands.*

GOOD READING

José Luis Concepción (1984), *The Guanches – survivors and their descendents* (Ediciones Graficolor, La Laguna).
Felipe Fernández-Armesto (1982), *The Canary Islands After the Conquest* (Clarendon, Oxford).
José Manuel Moreno (1994), *Fauna of Tenerife* (Ediciones Turquesa, Santa Cruz).
Lázaro Sánchez-Pinto and Lucas de Saá (1993), *Flora of the Canary Islands* (Ediciones Turquesa, Santa Cruz).
Ann and Larry Walker, *Pleasures of the Canary Islands: Wine, Food, Beauty, Mystery.*

▼ *Below: The easy ramble around Los Roques is the most popular walk in the national park.*

Be prepared to stand in a long queue in order to board the cable car – a two-hour wait is not unusual, so come early in the morning. The cable car runs from 09:00–16:00, with the last car leaving the top station at 16:50. Note that the cable car may not run in icy or windy conditions. There is a bar-restaurant at the lower cable car station that is open 09:00–17:00.

Visitors should also be aware that the car park at the cable car station can become seriously overcrowded – another good reason to arrive early; tel: 922 01 04 40, www.telefericoteide.com

Parador Las Cañadas del Teide ★

The road now crosses a low pass, the **Puerto de las Cañadas** at a height of 2300m (7546ft), dropping down southwards until the **Parador Las Cañadas del Teide** appears on the left. This is the only accommodation within the park boundaries and makes an excellent base for a few days' walking. It has a restaurant and shop that are open to the public and alongside there is a small Tourist Information Centre, with basic displays and literature on the geology and wildlife of the park. Note that the area around the Parador can become

◀ *Left: The Roques de García may be part of a volcanic dyke or the remains of an old crater wall.*

crowded with coach parties. Nearby is a small hermitage, the **Ermita de las Nieves**.

Visitors should note that the parador is very popular and is often fully booked. To ensure accommodation and avoid disappointment, it would be best to book ahead; tel/fax: 922 38 64 15, www.parador.es It is well worth the effort – watching the sun rise and set on the snow-capped peak of Mount Teide is one of the most evocative experiences you can have in the Canary Islands.

Roques de García ★★

Almost opposite the hermitage are the most photographed features of the park, the **Roques de García**, a series of strangely eroded volcanic rocks. The origin of the rocks is debatable. One suggestion is that they are part of an old crater wall, while another, more plausible theory is that they are part of a dyke or layer of hard intrusive igneous rock.

The most impressive of the rocks is the **Roque Chinchado**, which rises to a height of 30m (98ft) from a narrow base. This startling shape used to feature on the old 1000 peseta Spanish banknote (before the currency was replaced by the euro).

From the Roques de García there is a fine view over the **Llano de Ucanca**, the most westerly of the *cañadas*. Look

---

IDENTIFYING YOUR POLICEMEN

Hopefully, visitors to Tenerife will not need to contact a policeman – which is just as well, because, confusingly, there are three different police forces operating in Spain. Firstly, there are the **Policía Municipal**, who wear blue uniforms and carry out minor duties such as parking and traffic control. Secondly, there are the **Policía Nacional**, who have brown uniforms, and it is to this group that you should go if you are robbed or burgled. Finally, there are the **Guardia Civil**, who wear light green uniforms and who in the past were easily identified by their shiny black hats. Once greatly feared, the Guardia Civil have a less important role in modern democratic Spain. All Spanish police are armed and not noted for their sense of humour. It is not a good idea to adopt a frivolous approach towards them!

MOUNT TEIDE NATIONAL PARK

▲ *Above: Hiking on one of the lower forest paths near Mount Teide.*

for the rocks known as **Los Azulejos** – they are stained jade green by the iron and copper in the strata. Another strange rock formation here is the **Zapato de la Reina** (the Queen's Shoe), which resembles a high-heeled shoe. The road through the park finally reaches the western end at **Boca de Tauce**.

Be prepared for crowds at the Roques del García. This is a regular stop for the tourist coaches and there can be hundreds of people swarming along the paths (which are becoming seriously eroded in places) and on the viewing terraces. Late afternoon, when the tourist coaches have gone, is probably the best time to appreciate the magnificence of the Roques.

CLIMBING MOUNT TEIDE

From the main road through the national park a climb to the top of Mount Teide looks easy enough, but this is deceptive and it should only be attempted by serious and well-equipped hikers. The usual route to the summit starts from a car park situated on the main road approximately 2km (1.25 miles) east of the cable car station. The track is well defined, but because of the loose nature of the surface material and the thin air at this altitude, the hike can be exhausting.

The route heads first for **Montaña Blanca** – named after the white pumice lying around there – and then proceeds upwards in a series of broad curves. Look out for **Los Huevos del Teide** (the Eggs of Teide), which are huge, rounded, black volcanic rocks.

At a height of around 3260m (10,696ft) the track reaches the **Altavista mountain hut**. Many climbers spend the night at this refuge in order to be able to see the sunrise from the peak (permits are not required for sunrise ascents), which can be quite a magical experience. The hut is open in the summer months only. You can book a place in this shelter (tel: 922 01 04 40). Uphill from the hut it is worth making a diversion to the **Cueva del Hielo** (the Ice Cave), which is festooned with icicles throughout the year.

Once you have returned to the main path, a further 20 minutes' walk brings you to **La Rambleta**, where the upper cable car station is located. From here it takes another 20 minutes up the **Pan de Azúcar** (Sugar Loaf) to reach the crater rim, passing along the way some smoking fumeroles, where for the greater part of the year it is comforting to warm your hands in the hot vapours. The summit is usually in full sunlight even though it may be cloudy further below. The views can be stupendous and from here you can pick out the islands of Gran Canaria, El Hierro, La Gomera and La Palma, as well as large parts of Tenerife. The total climb is around 1500m (4920ft) and should take between three and four hours.

Some words of warning: Don't think of attempting the climb in inclement weather; don't ever climb alone; make sure that you are well equipped; check the prevailing weather conditions at the El Portillo visitors' centre; and always remember that oxygen is in short supply on the summit, so forget the whole idea if you have respiratory problems.

Visitors who are physically fit but who are inexperienced in mountain walking are strongly advised to join a guided group organized by the National Park staff. Book well in advance by calling ICONA (tel: 922 92 23 71). Alternatively, it is possible to book at their office at Calle Dr Sixto Perera Gonzalez 24, El Mayorazgo, La Orotava. Open Monday–Friday 09:00–14:00.

SAND FAR FROM THE BEACH

Visitors are often surprised to see large areas of sand in the Mount Teide National Park. This phenomenon has been caused by **weathering**. Low temperatures at night, when the numbers drop down to below freezing point, are contrasted with very high temperatures during the day, when readings often rise to above 38°C (100°F) on the south-facing slopes. This causes stress in the rocks, causing them to break down into granules in their constituent mineral parts. This process is called **mechanical weathering**. The best place in the Mount Teide National Park to see a large expanse of weathered sand is in the area known as Arenas Blanca ('White Sand'), which is located just to the south of the main road going through the park. Here, the wind has actually blown the weathered material into dunes that give the impression of a mini-Sahara.

MOUNT TEIDE NATIONAL PARK

OTHER WALKS IN THE PARK

The visitors' centre offers a total of nine guided walks varying in degrees of difficulty and lasting between 30 minutes and six hours. It is essential to book these guided walks in advance by telephoning ICONA (tel: 922 92 23 71). In addition, there is a network of walking trails that can be used by walkers independently, some of which are signposted and have stopping points with information boards.

There is one special route that has been designed with handicapped people in mind. Walkers should remember that they are not allowed to stray from the marked trails.

Information Boards

Possibly the most impressive aspect of a visit to the Mount Teide National Park are the numerous information boards that appear in a variety of places. The boards usually have a labelled sketch that mirrors the view in front of the observer. The scenery is then described and explained in both Spanish and English, so that the visitor without even a basic knowledge of geology can appreciate and understand the scenery.

THE WILDLIFE OF LAS CAÑADAS DEL TEIDE

◀ *Left: One of the many information boards that offer visitors a description of the park's scenery.*

◀◀ *Opposite: A mobile shop touts for business at a viewpoint just outside the national park.*

It is easy, for example, to distinguish between acid and basic lavas, to make an educated guess at the varying age of the lavas depending on the amount of vegetation that has begun to grow on their surfaces, and to differentiate between a dyke and a sill. The information board at the western end of the national park near Boca de Tauce is particularly helpful.

THE WILDLIFE OF LAS CAÑADAS DEL TEIDE
Fauna
Mammals are shy and elusive in the park and only **rabbits** are likely to be seen. **Mouflon** were introduced to the park in 1971, but research has shown that they have a detrimental effect on the native plants, so their numbers are now being culled. As a result they are extremely shy and very cautious. **Bats** can be seen at dusk and the occasional Canarian **lizard** may be observed basking on a rock.

There are plenty of birds in evidence. The most common bird is the small, brown and unobtrusive **Berthalot's pipit**, which can often be seen in small groups around the parador. Look skyward for **plain swifts** and **buzzards**, while **Great**

THE GIANT BUGLOSS

Mount Teide National Park is noted for its remarkable flora, with a number of species which are endemic not only to Tenerife, but to the park itself. Pride of place goes to the **giant bugloss** (*Echium wildpretii*) known in Spanish as the *Tajinaste rojo*, with tall red flower spikes that can reach up to 2m (6.5ft) in height. It flowers in May, but later in the year the dead flower heads can look equally attractive. The rare **Teide violet** (*Viola cheirathifolia*) was discovered by Humboldt in the 19th century. It can be seen on the highest parts of the park, where it flowers after the snows have melted. One of the most abundant plants in the park is the **Teide broom** (*Spartocytisus supranubius*), a hemispherical shaped bush with aromatic pink and white flowers blooming in late spring and early summer.

MOUNT TEIDE NATIONAL PARK

Grey Shrikes are often seen, sitting on telephone wires and other prominent perches. At lower levels, especially at the forest picnic sites, the **blue chaffinch**, indigenous to Tenerife, can be very tame. **Butterflies** can be common, particularly during the spring, with the **Canary blue**, **monarch** and **painted lady** most likely to be fluttering past.

Flora

Despite the great height and the aridity of the landscape, a surprising range of wild flowers proliferates in the park, including 45 endemic species. The star of the show is the enormous **giant bugloss** (*Echium wildpretii* or *Tajinaste rojo*), which has a red floral spike that can be around 2m (6.5ft) in length. Other endemics include the **Teide violet**, which was discovered by von Humboldt, the **Teide daisy** and the **Teide broom**.

Remember that it is forbidden to collect rocks, plants and animals. It is also prohibited to light fires, camp overnight and use any roads or tracks that are not open to the public. Needless to say, it is against regulations to leave litter in the park.

▼ *Below: The only vegetation that survives in the national park must be able to cope with the arid climate and an acid soil.*

BEST TIMES TO VISIT

The park can be spectacular in **winter**, when there is often deep snow, but this can lead to problems of access, as footpaths may be closed, roads blocked and the cable car may not be running.

In the summer the park may be crowded and there may be long delays on the cable car. **Spring** is probably the best time to visit, with the wild flowers at their best and a capping of snow on the higher parts of the mountain. Whatever time you visit, come early and, if possible, choose a clear day.

GETTING THERE

There is one bus a day from Los Cristianos and Playa de las Américas and one bus a day from Puerto de la Cruz. For most people, therefore, a **coach** excursion or a **hire car** will be the most appropriate way of getting there. It is possible to hire a taxi, but this will be an expensive way of seeing the park.

GETTING AROUND

There is no public transport within the park, so if you do not wish to be at the mercy of a coach driver, a hire car is the only option. Many people **cycle** around the park, although how they have the energy for this

exercise after climbing 3000m (10,000ft) is a mystery!

WHERE TO STAY

No camping is allowed within the Mount Teide National Park. The only formal accommodation option is at the: **Parador Las Cañadas del Teide**, tel: 922 38 64 15, fax: 922 38 23 52, www.parador.es While this is an expensive option, it is in a marvellous setting and once the tour coaches have gone there is the mouth-watering prospect of watching the sun set on the snow-capped peak. Traditional Canarian food.

WHERE TO EAT

There is a restaurant and a snack bar at the Parador. There are also snack bars at the upper and lower cable car stations. A number of popular restaurants are located around the Visitors' Centre at El Portillo. It is a good idea to bring your own picnic lunch as there are a number of purpose-built picnic sites both in and around the fringes of the national park.

USEFUL CONTACTS

There are **Tourist Information Centres** at: **El Portillo** at the eastern

end of the park and also at the **Parador**. Both have information regarding whether hiking trails are open and the cable car is running. The park is administered from La Orotava and staff can be contacted at Calle Doctor Sixto Perera González 25, tel: 922 92 23 71, www.ma grama.gob.es

Cable Car:

It is important to check if the cable car is running. It can frequently close down because of wind, snow or maintenance. For more information, tel: 922 01 04 45, www.telefericoteide.com

Travel Agencies:

The following travel agencies organize excursions to Mount Teide: From Los Cristianos/Playa de las Américas: Tenerife Sunshine Travel Centre, Avenida Amsterdam, tel: 922 75 18 67, www.tenerifesunshine.com or Tenerife Excursions, Calle Rodeo, tel: 922 75 33 63, www.tenerife-excursions. co.uk For private tours, Orange bus transfers can organise bespoke trips. Contact Office 3, Arrivals Hall, Reina Sofia Airport (Airport South), tel: 922 79 11 14, www.orangebus.eu

Travel Tips

Tourist Information

The **Spanish Tourist Board** has offices in the USA (New York, Beverly Hills, Chicago, Miami), Canada (Toronto) and several non-English speaking countries. In the UK (also for the Republic of Ireland), the address is: Spanish National Tourist Office, 6th Floor, 64 North Row, London W1K 7DE, tel: 020 317 2040, www.tour-spain.co.uk

There are Tourist Board offices (ask for the *Oficina de Turismo*) in many places on Tenerife. The largest are: **Santa Cruz**, Plaza de España, tel: 922 23 95 92; **Puerto de la Cruz**, Casa de la Aduana, tel: 922 38 60 00, fax: 38 47 69; **Playa de las Américas**, town centre, tel: 922 79 76 68, fax: 75 71 98; **Los Cristianos**, Town Hall, tel: 922 75 71 37, fax: 75 71 38; and **Reina Sofía Airport**, tel: 922 39 20 37. Staff usually speak English and provide brochures, timetables and help with car rental and accommodation. The official website for the island is www.webtenerife.co.uk Other useful websites include: www.destinationtenerife.com and www.realtenerifeislanddrives.com

Entry Requirements

Visitors from Britain, Canada, USA, New Zealand and Australia must have a valid passport. Those staying more than three months will require a visa from the Spanish embassy in their native country. Visa extensions on Tenerife must be applied for at the Gobierno Civil in Santa Cruz. Anyone arriving by ferry with their own car will need a driving licence and the international insurance Green Card.

Customs

The duty-free allowance is: alcohol: one litre spirits, two litres fortified wine and two litres table wine; tobacco: 200 cigarettes or 50 cigars; gifts: up to the value of £390.

Health Requirements

No vaccinations are necessary unless coming from a country with smallpox, typhoid or yellow fever. There is no malaria and mosquitoes are rare. Visitors from EU countries should bring their EU Health Card – this will gain them some degree of free medical treatment, but is no substitute for a good medical insurance.

Getting There

By Air: Cheap charter flights go from many European countries direct to Tenerife. Many scheduled flights (more expensive) go via Madrid. From North America, Australia and South Africa, the Madrid route is the only option. A number of **'no-frills' airlines** run regular scheduled services to Tenerife, including **Ryanair**, which operates from twelve UK airports and others in Eire and on the European mainland (www.ryanair.com); **EasyJet** runs flights to Tenerife from Bristol, Newcastle, Southend, Manchester and London Gatwick (www.easyjet.com); and **Monarch** has flights from London Luton, London Gatwick, Birmingham, East Midlands, Leeds Bradford and Manchester. International flights arrive at Reina Sofía (Tenerife South), in the south, which can be very busy at peak times. There are car-hire facilities. Taxis reach Playa de las Américas in about 20 minutes and Puerto de la Cruz in 1 hour 45 minutes. Regular buses run south to all the main resorts and north to Santa Cruz.

By Ship: The only ferry from Europe to Tenerife is the **Trasmediterránea** ship which comes from Cádiz on mainland Spain. It runs once a week to Santa Cruz and stops at Las Palmas in Gran Canaria en route. Book well in advance for summer sailings; tel: 902 45 46 45, www.trasmediterranea.es

What to Pack

With a mild climate year-round, there is no need to pack heavy clothing. A light jumper and windproof jacket are useful for evenings or trips to the mountains. For beach holidays, light sandals are recommended as the volcanic sand can become very hot underfoot. Stronger footwear is needed for hiking in the mountains. The sun can be strong all year, so sunglasses and sun hat are recommended. Light cotton clothes, shorts, swimming costumes and sun protection creams are essential for most holiday-makers. Ladies will find a sarong useful. Take smarter casual clothing for the evenings, particularly in hotels and expensive restaurants. Beachwear is unacceptable in churches. Canarians usually dress casually, except for formal occasions. Tenerife is highly photogenic and most visitors will bring a camera or camcorder. Spare films are readily available. If you should forget to pack an essential item, all is not lost. The tourist resorts have shops that sell clothing, beachwear, sports gear and books in various languages.

MONEY MATTERS

Currency: The euro (€) is divided into 100 cents. Coins come in denominations of 1, 2, 5, 10, 20 and 50 cents. Notes are issued in 5, 10, 50, 100, 200 and 500 euros.

Currency exchange: Travellers' cheques and foreign currency can be cashed at banks, change outlets, post offices and hotels. Have your passport ready when cashing travellers' cheques.

Banks: Finding a bank is not a problem, although service may be slow. They are open on weekdays, 09:00–14:00; on Saturdays, 09:00–13:00. They will charge a small commission cashing travellers' cheques, but will usually give a better rate of

exchange than other places.
Credit Cards: Major credit cards are accepted in most shops, hotels, restaurants and exchange offices. There are automatic cash dispensers in the larger towns and resorts, using a variety of languages.
Tipping: A service charge is added to hotel and restaurant bills, so tipping is a matter of personal choice. A small gratuity can be paid for good service. Taxi drivers, guides and porters will expect a tip (*una propina*) of 5–10 per cent. There is no VAT in Tenerife, but there is a special Canary Island tax (IGIC) of 7 per cent on retail goods and services, which will be included in all bills and prices.

ACCOMMODATION
Most accommodation is geared to package tours, which means that the individual traveller who just turns up will usually find that the hotel or apartment is fully booked. It is best to book before arriving. There is a range of hotels from luxury five-star establishments to modest one-star pensions. Aparthotels have the usual facilities, but will have some self-catering rooms. State-run *paradores* are usually located in historic buildings, have traditional furniture and specialize in local food. Apartments far outnumber hotels and are usually cheaper. They normally have similar facilities (pools, bars, restaurants). Most apartments are self-catering, but a variety of food can be sampled in local restaurants. There are several

official camp sites. To use them you need a permit. *Casas rurales* are converted farmhouses or village properties, an option for those wishing to get away from the bustle of the large resorts; advance booking is essential. For details, contact local tourist offices, visit www.ecoturismocanarias.com or phone Rural Tenerife on 922 08 50 15. Tenerife is a year-round destination, with a high season from December to March when the climate is attractive to northern Europeans. At this time the accommodation is at its most expensive and most likely to be fully booked. Summer is also busy, when mainland Spaniards come to Tenerife. Low-season prices for accommodation tend to be in May and November.

EATING OUT
Restaurants in the resort areas cater mainly for tourists and generally provide international food. Usually there is a printed

menu posted outside, often with a national flag, and sometimes photographs of the food. **Fast-food** restaurants abound, such as KFC, McDonalds and numerous pizza places. Food from Italy, Thailand, India, China, France and Mexico ensures a wide choice. For **Canarian food**, head inland or to Santa Cruz. Lunch rarely starts before 14:00 and the evening meal around 19:30. Sample the many **fish restaurants** providing a variety of fresh shellfish (*mariscos*) and fish (*pescado*), usually at a reasonable price. **Cafés** and **bars** are everywhere and many provide *tapas* with the drinks. Cheapest is to order the meal of the day (*menú del día*), usually a starter, main course, pudding and drink. Two useful websites are: www. tenerife-restaurants-guide.com and www.tenerifedining.com

TRANSPORT

Air: Inter-island flights with Binter Airlaines go from Tenerife to all the other Canary Islands. Most leave from Los Rodeos Airport in the north. Tel: 902 39 13 92, www.binter

canarias.com
Ferries: All the islands are served by regular ferries, mostly Naviera Armas or Lineas Fred Olsen.
Buses: Known as *guaguas*, buses provide a comprehensive service around the island. Most are run by the TITSA company and are green in colour. Bus stops (or *paradas*) are marked by a large sign with the letter P. Visitors should consider buying a Bonobus card, which gives a 25 per cent discount on tickets.
Car Hire: Rates are very reasonable and with a good, well-signposted road system, a car rental can add much to the enjoyment of a holiday. Most international rental firms have offices at the airport. Although in theory an International Driving Permit (IDP) is required, in practice most firms accept a valid national driving licence.
Driving Hints: In Tenerife you drive on the right, overtake on the left and give way on round abouts to traffic already there. Carry your **driving licence** and passport (or a photocopy)

when driving as the police can demand to see them. **Seat belts** should be worn at all times, including rear seats. It is prohibited to use a mobile phone when driving and to throw objects out of the car window. The **blood alcohol limit** is 0.08 per cent and any driver involved in an accident can expect to be breathalyzed, so it is sensible not to drink alcohol if driving. Police can impose on-the-spot fines to non-resident drivers, but there is a 20 per cent discount if paid immediately. Visitors bringing their own car will need an IDP, car registration papers, a nationality sticker, a Green Card extension to the insurance policy and a red warning triangle in case of a breakdown. Spectacle wearers must carry a spare pair. Speed limits are 120kph (75mph) on motorways, 100kph (62mph) on dual carriageways and 90kph (55mph) on other roads. The speed limit in built-up areas is 50kph (31mph). A motorway (*autopista*) runs two-thirds of the way around the island, from Adeje in the southwest to Los Realjos in the north. It is possible to drive all the way around Tenerife in a day. Progress on inland roads, however, can be slow, owing to rough surfaces and hairpin bends. **Parking** in the larger towns and cities can be difficult and it is best to use the underground car parks where provided. Pay and display areas are marked with blue lines. Cars parked illegally are quickly towed away and can be expensive, time-consuming and frustrating to recover.

CONVERSION CHART

From	To	Multiply By
Millimetres	Inches	0.0394
Metres	Yards	1.0936
Metres	Feet	3.281
Kilometres	Miles	0.6214
Square kilometres	Square miles	0.386
Hectares	Acres	2.471
Litres	Pints	1.760
Kilograms	Pounds	2.205
Tonnes	Tons	0.984

To convert Celsius to Fahrenheit: x 9 ÷ 5 + 32

In the event of an accident involving a hire car, report the incident to the hire firm immediately. Petrol stations are widespread and most accept credit cards. Fuel is cheaper than in Spain and the rest of Europe. Tourist offices can provide adequate maps, but for more detail try bookshops. New Holland's Globetrotter Map of Tenerife is highly recommended.

Taxis: Tenerife's taxis are good value. They are generally white Mercedes showing a plate with the letters SP (*Servicio Público* – Public Service). For short journeys they are metered, but for longer journeys negotiate a fare with the driver. A green roof light means the taxi is available.

Trains: There are no trains in the Canary Islands, although an electric tram links La Laguna with Santa Cruz.

BUSINESS HOURS

Offices, post offices and most shops open 09:00–13:00. After the siesta period, they re-open from 15:00–19:00. Saturday opening is 09:00–13:00. Food stores and supermarkets may open for longer periods, while some shops in the tourist resorts may open on Sundays.

TIME DIFFERENCE

Tenerife maintains GMT in the winter months, so there is a one-hour time difference with the continent. Clocks go back one hour during the summer.

COMMUNICATIONS

Telephones: The old three-figure regional digits have now been incorporated into the telephone numbers, so you have to dial all nine numbers even if phoning within the same town. For an international call, dial 00 and the country code, followed by the area code (omitting the first 0) and then the number. If dialling Tenerife from abroad, the country code is 34, the same as the rest of Spain. There are many blue telephone booths, which take both phone cards and cash. Phone cards (*tarjetas telefónicas*) can be bought at post offices and tobacconists. Many cafés and bars also have public telephones, but these are more expensive than those on the street. The police emergency number is **091**. Visitors should have no difficulty using their **mobile phones** in Tenerife, as service providers automatically lock in to local suppliers.

Internet and WiFi: Most hotels offer access for guests. WiFi hot-spots are available in bars and cafés in the tourist areas.

Post: Post boxes are yellow. Stamps (*sellos*) are sold at post offices (*oficinas de correos*), newsagents and shops that sell postcards. Post offices open at normal office hours. The postal service is slow. Allow a week for a card to reach Europe, 10 days for North America and 14 days for Australia or New Zealand.

Fax: Most hotels will provide a fax service free of charge, but expect to pay a small charge for the service in a post office or tourist information centre.

ELECTRICITY

The current in Tenerife is 220V, though some hotels have 110V sockets for shavers. Plugs have two round pins in line with most of Europe. Bring adapters for appliances as you will not be able to buy them in Tenerife.

ROAD SIGNS

Alto • Stop
Camino cerrado • Road closed
Ceda el paso • Give way
Circunvalación • Bypass
Curva peligrosa • Dangerous bend
Derecha • Right
Derecho • Straight on
Despacio • Slow
Derrumbes en la vía • Rockfalls on the road
Dirección unica • One way
Izquierdo • Left
No adelantar • No overtaking
No estacionar • No parking
No hay paso • No entrance
Peligro • Danger
Reduzca velocidad • Reduce speed
Salida • Exit
Semáforo • Traffic lights
Trabajos en la vía • Roadworks

WEIGHTS AND MEASURES

The metric system is used both in Tenerife and the rest of the Canary Islands.

HEALTH SERVICES

Citizens of EU countries are entitled to free medical treatment on production of Form E111 or the new EU Health Card (obtain before travelling). This does not, however, cover prescriptions and dental treatment and is no substitute for a good **travel insurance policy** covering medical treatment.

TRAVEL TIPS

Tenerife has five good hospitals and a host of private clinics. Hotels can usually provide the name of an English-speaking **doctor** (*médico*). For minor medical problems, go to a **chemist** (*farmacia*). Pharmacists in Spain give advice and are allowed to dispense a variety of prescription drugs. *Farmacias* are open during normal shop hours and are distinguished by an illuminated green cross. In a large town, at least one will be open after hours and a duty rota shown in the window. The Red Cross (*Cruz Roja*) often have small medical centres in kiosks on beaches in the main resorts. Services for **disabled travellers** are much improved. The airport, larger hotels and many tourist attractions are more aware these days of wheelchair requirements. The resort of Los Cristianos has a very good reputation for wheelchair provision. It is advisable, however, to warn airlines and hotels of any special needs well in advance. For information, try www.tourismforall.org.uk or tel: 0845 124 9971.

Health Precautions

Visitors will experience few problems. Hygiene requirements are strict, so food poisoning is rare. The biggest danger is **sunburn** and **dehydration**. Use sun block, wear a hat and good sunglasses and avoid exposure during the hottest parts of the day. It is possible for the skin to be burnt even when there is a layer of cloud. To avoid dehydration take plenty of non-alcoholic liquids. The main symptoms of heatstroke are nausea, headaches and increased heartbeats. Treat initially with rehydration solutions containing sugar, salt and water. Tap water in the main resorts is usually good, but less reliable in rural areas. The water is fine for brushing teeth, but **bottled water** (*agua mineral*) is advised for drinking. The fizzy version is *agua con gas* and the still variety *agua sin gas*. Another cause of illness is too much **alcohol**. Non-alcoholic beer (*cerveza sin alcohol*) is widely available, even on draught. There is no malaria in Tenerife, but mosquitoes and other biting **insects** can be a nuisance. Use insect repellent, especially in the evenings.

Personal Safety

Crime is relatively low – the police keep a high profile. Most visitors will never feel threatened, but petty crime does exist, mainly bag snatching and theft from cars. Take a few simple precautions. Keep valuables in the hotel or apartment security boxes. Do not leave valuable articles in your car or take expensive belongings to the beach. Avoid badly lit areas at night. Keep cash in a body belt or pouch. Lock hotel windows and balconies. Beware of pickpockets in crowded places such as bus stations and markets. Keep photocopies of passports and driving licences. If you are the victim of a crime, report it to the police immediately and get a signed statement to present to your insurance company.

Emergencies

To contact the **police** call **091**. Alternatively, use the pan-European emergency number **112** for all emergencies to reach English speaking staff.

Etiquette

Topless sunbathing is a feature at beaches and pools, but full nudity is only tolerated at certain official locations. Beachwear is not acceptable when visiting churches and cathedrals.

Language

The official language of Tenerife is **Castilian Spanish**, but the dialect is similar to that spoken in Andalucía or South America. English is also widely spoken.

INDEX

INDEX